COACHING
YOUR WAY TO SUCCESS

The process for leading an innovative business.

Donna M. Capobianco, Ph.D.

How the Process Works

This book is about a very simple, highly effective way to manage an aggressive, growth-oriented business, where innovation and change are the norm. When embraced top down by any team, it works.

The process described here has been thoroughly tested over more than twenty years. It has been applied in companies of varying sizes, representing many industries including financial services, communication, manufacturing, and retail. All the businesses shared some common factors: they were all highly innovative, experiencing aggressive growth and all were going through major transitions at the time they implemented the process. Size was relevant only in the time it took to implement.

When this system is fully utilized, positive results are normally evident within ninety days of implementation and continue as long as the process is in use.

Adopting this method clears the path for innovation implementation and organizational re-structuring, facilitates cultural change, enhances and targets company communication, and greatly simplifies record keeping. From a human resource perspective, the method significantly reduces unhealthy turnover, improves employee relations while reducing legal claims and greatly simplifies hiring, training, management development, information systems and reporting. There are only four basic, one-page, easily programmable forms required to make it work. The four forms minimize training needs and improve record keeping, data collection, and time management. All this contributes to moving through your next change faster, while actually making the life of all end users, everyone in the organization to one degree or another, more pleasant. Some of the key potential domino effects of implementing the process are increased performance, decreased turnover and a cultural shift to expect and be ready for the next innovation.

The book walks you through a management process using a "read and do" coaching platform. Coaching is the most productive and enjoyable way to achieve higher levels of success. Managers who coach their teams as part of their daily routine know that to be personally successful, their people must excel. Good coaching is the most powerful tool a manager can use. There is no better or easier alternative. We see the results or lack of it so easily in sports. Applying good coaching to business is no different.

If you love complex models or the latest craze in highly evolved management philosophy, you do not want to read any further. However, if you like things simple, can tolerate straightforward, plain talk that everyone in your organization can understand, are willing to be refreshed on or take a new view of the management process, and then help your management team actually teach and coach to the process, please be my guest and proceed.

To implement:

1. Expect all levels of management to read the book and implement the process within thirty to sixty days, using the four critical forms.

2. Expect senior management to coach to the process.

3. Provide coaching training and support to senior management to hone their skills utilizing professionally trained coaches as needed.

4. Begin measuring results by looking at quantity and quality of forms completed:

   • Thirty days: *Performance Expectation Sheets* completed for all positions.

   • Sixty days: *Recruiting & Hiring Worksheets* on file for each position.

   • Sixty days: *Performance Review Form* completed and on file for each review occurrence.

   • Ninety days: *Performance Improvement Action Plans* in every employee's HR file.

5. Teach to and provide continuous coaching at all levels of the management team, integrating coaching in your corporate culture.

For as long as the process is embraced and coached to by all levels of management, the process works.

It is all about how good we are at bringing others forward to meet the demands of innovation and changing expectations. The coaching method described in this book focuses on three management success factors that make that happen:

1. Recruiting and hiring the best people for the job.

2. Training and coaching all to meet the performance expectations of the job.

3. Conducting performance reviews often, fairly, positively, and on time.

The ability to perform all three critical success factors has a direct impact on each work team's ability to move through the challenges of innovation and change. Senior managers who buy in and are willing to learn will very likely find something to increase their effectiveness at helping all individuals in the organization reach their greatest potential.

If your management team can embrace, practice, and be coached along to perform these success factors well, your company will quickly see considerably higher results and significantly lower resistance to change. Also, your team will be reminded or gain awareness of some legal considerations for carrying out the process responsibly and ethically.

Exercises are provided along the way to help build and test understanding. Repetition is built in to enhance learning. Your entire management team can begin to practice the method immediately after reading. They should expect to receive coaching from senior managers, HR professionals, and trained professional coaches to help integrate the process more quickly.

Although each person on the management team brings their own personality and style, all involved must employ the process taught in this book. If embraced and implemented, the simple message that lies within these pages becomes self-evident.

Management's job is to set reasonable expectations, train and coach to those expectations, and measure and communicate along the way to reaching them.

We succeed if our people succeed.

Prepare to Coach by Knowing What You Need

Prepare by knowing and documenting the performance expectations of each job and how each directly contributes to the company reaching its overall goal. Performance expectations state what is expected in a job and how it will be measured. This part may take a little time to get done, so let's take it step by step. We are going into depth on performance expectations, as it is the foundation of this management team and coaching model.

Performance expectations are valuable to everyone on the team:

- Simple measurable expectations are the single greatest contributor to a positive work environment (people like open communication and knowing what is expected of them).

- Every job has responsibilities and every responsibility has a measurable minimum expectation associated with carrying it out (its standard of performance).

- Clear expectations simplify and enhance everybody's job by helping to prioritize responsibilities and make them measurable, objective, consistent, open, and easy to communicate.

When senior mangement has clear expectations, they stand a bettter chance of successfully directing and coaching the managers and team leaders reporting to them. Performance expectations apply only to behavior and attitude that is job-related, observable, and measurable. They should be based on average achievable performance (what the average steady good performers do) or on the customer's expectations (i.e., same-day response to calls, courteous and knowledgeable service people, etc.). If expectations are set and all management, senior on down, adopts this coaching method, your average performance will likely well exceed the best performance of your competitors. That is, of course, until your competitors start using the process you are now learning.

Performance expectations include attendance and attitude. Excellent attendance ensures each member of the team is pulling her/his weight. It also shows a respect for the team and respect for the importance of one's own work. Meeting or exceeding team goals requires *every* member of the team meeting or exceeding her/his own goals *every* day. Your company's policy regarding attendance should reinforce this concept.

Most managers expect to see behavior that represents a positive, helpful attitude toward the job and the team. Behavior expresses attitude. Negative behavior only serves to hold back progress and pull down morale. Negative attitudes are often the single greatest contributor to poor team performance. Keeping the team focused on positive behavior is also one of the greatest challenges of a manager.

When it comes to attitude, setting expectations that lead to appropriate team interaction and communication can be helpful. This is not about everyone being friendly or winning popularity contests. It is about having consistent expectations that are to be upheld by all members of the team, including, and most importantly, the manager. In order to keep expectations consistent and simple, they must be easily observable and understandable by all. There are three attitude expectations most successful work teams adhere to and uphold.

Everyone on the team has the right to:

- Be heard

- Be treated respectfully

- Express ideas

Lastly, when considering setting or changing expectations, the achievement of the expectations must be within the control of the individual. If something occurs outside of the individual's control that impacts her/his ability to meet any expectations, the manager and team may need to assist to ensure control is placed back with the employee so expectations can be met and the work can get done.

> *EXAMPLE: A company's service department employs seven service specialists. Each of the seven service specialists is assigned a group of approximately twenty locations to support. The location contacts are office managers, and in the office manager's absence, operations managers. Each group of twenty locations normally averages similar numbers of service calls and research requests. A responsibility or performance*

expectation for all service specialists is to achieve an 8+ rating for call response time. This is measured via quarterly customer satisfaction surveys (rating scale is 1-10, where 10 is the highest score).

The manager received two separate location complaints about one service specialist's response time. This service specialist's rating on response time has consistently been 9.5 or better, and no customer has ever called in before with a complaint about this person. Coincidentally, this same service specialist had requested to meet with the manager that same day to gain some help on solving a problem. They were scheduled to meet that afternoon. When investigating, the manager learned three locations in this service specialist's group just hired new office managers and two locations have new operations managers and no office managers. When new contacts are in the first few weeks of their learning curve they often call two and three times a day for help. Normally, a specialist hears from a location only once or twice a week (five locations out of twenty were causing a temporary volume surge).

The service specialist needed help in finding a temporary solution to ensure the "call response time" service standard could continue to be met while these five new contacts were in their learning curve. The service specialist lost the ability to meet the standard through no fault of her own and needed the manager and team's help to ensure expectations would be met.

If performance expectations are new to your team, it is important to implement them slowly and carefully. Start by asking your team to participate in writing down what work or service levels must be accomplished in your department and by when. Examples might include:

- All invoices must be paid in the week they are submitted.

- All orders must be processed by 3 p.m. Wednesday.

- Reach sales revenue of $2 million by end of first quarter.

- Maintain 2% or less error rate.

When you have work items that are predictable and countable, simply divide the average number of each by the number of people doing that job on a full-time basis to arrive at the average standard for that time period. Work with the shortest but most reasonable time periods (per hour, per day, per week).

- 4,000 invoices a week on average / 7 A/P clerks = 571 invoices processed per clerk per week

- 1,200 orders processed on average daily / 5 order entry reps = 240 orders per rep per day

- $2 mil. annual sales revenue / 8 reps = $250,000 per rep / 50 weeks = $5,000 per rep per week

Some expectations are best measured by how your customers rate your performance. For instance, if your customers expect same-day response to their calls, then your expectation for all service representatives might be a 9+ customer satisfaction rating for response time. The rating can be determined by a monthly customer satisfaction survey using a rating scale of 1-10, 10 being the highest score.

Doing the management job effectively means constantly looking at the workload and tasks you have assigned each person to ensure relative equality. Keep a watch for changes in workload that may affect the individual's ability to perform to standard and make adjustments as needed to keep the work spread evenly. Adjust expectations only when necessary and teach your team to expect changes that keep performance in line with meeting and exceeding ever-changing company or department goals.

Expectations based upon what is consistently accomplished by the few top or superstar performers would be unreasonable to expect from everyone. It is also unwise to set expectations based on what the lowest-level performers do. After all, no manager wants to decrease chances of reaching goals. And no manager wants to increase expenses by having to hire more low-level performers to get the job done.

The amount of time each member of the team needs to achieve standard performance is also very important. New hires usually experience a period of learning before they can perform at standard. Managers who know, on average, what that learning time period is, can be very helpful to a new hire by communicating:

- The expectations of the job and which ones apply immediately (certain expectations, like attendance and attitude, apply from the start).

- Which expectations have a learning period and the progress expected during that period.

- What training and assistance will be provided to ensure a new hire has the opportunity to reach expected performance in the normal time frame.

People most often do what they believe is expected and what they are rewarded most for. Doing the job becomes easier for all concerned when there are clearly communicated, consistent, controllable expectations and simple compensation programs that support those expectations.

Quantity expectations are tied to some number, like how much, how many, how often. Quality expectations relate to specific criteria or parameters on how the job is to be done, as in how good, how efficient, how flexible. Quantity and quality expectations go hand in hand.

Fulfilling many management responsibilities and reaching the overall goals of your department or company are contingent upon your team members fulfilling and achieving their responsibilities and goals. The expectations set for each job should be directly related to achieving the overall goals. If you discover a position that does not contribute in some meaningful way to meeting overall goals, consider eliminating it.

To get an idea of how to derive reasonable yet challenging performance expectations, let's look at an example of how one company's sales team does it.

Setting Expectations Case Study

It's now July and the Titletown Company has just finished with the budget process. Sales revenue this year was set at $1.7 million and increased to $2 million for next year's budget. Titletown's management desires to grow its revenue, its people, and its profit.

Currently there are seven established sales reps and two reps in training on the team. With sales revenue increasing next year to $2 million, the budget includes adding one sales rep. The sales manager is working now on hiring one new rep to be on board by October 1 this year. This will ensure the new hire will be able to meet the revenue standard by January 1. Sales rep turnover averages 20%. This means eight of the ten fully trained reps will each likely work at full capacity fifty weeks next year, given vacations and sick time.

Factoring in turnover, downtime, and a few other realistic shortfalls, Titletown's sales manager plans to reach budgeted goal by setting expected revenue performance next year at:

$5,000 per wk per rep (8 reps X $5,000 per wk X 50 wks worked = $2,000,000.

In order to grow and be profitable, the key responsibilities performed by each member of the team must be performed at or above a specific level or standard. To fulfill each responsibility, the specific level or expectation must be met. The sales manager knows how important it is to meet expectations, especially when it comes to sales revenue, good attendance, and team attitude. Also, accurate and timely reporting by each team member is crucial for determining day-to-day progress. By job type, each performance expectation set for every critical responsibility must be consistent, doable, measurable, and easy to communicate.

Following is a copy of Titletown's sales manager and sales representative responsibilities and performance expectations. Review these carefully and determine how they match up to the performance expectations you have associated with the responsibilities of your own position. Check to see if your key responsibilities and the expectations set for each are measurable, achievable, controllable, and easily understood. Then consider the same for each position you supervise. Verify the expectations are consistent, doable, measurable, easy to communicate, and can lead to your department/company's goals and desired results.

Performance Expectations for Sales Manager

Responsibilities   Quantity and Quality Performance Expectations

Attendance: Fewer than two late arrivals, early leaves or absences per quarter or fewer than five total per year. Illness or absence requiring additional time should be discussed with your manager or HR.

Attitude: Uphold in the workplace all team members' rights to:

- Be heard.

- Be treated respectfully.

- Express ideas.

Recruit and hire people who match the needs of the job: <15% turnover.

Train and coach to performance expectations of the job: All staff has Performance Improvement Action Plans in progress.

- Each staff member knows job expectations.

- 80% of non-trainee staff meet or exceed expectations.

Measure and communicate results to expectations: All staff:

- Know personal and overall team status to expectations.

- Can define how they are measured.

- Can tie compensation to performance expectations.

Conduct performance reviews: All reviews conducted within five business days of due date. Reviews conducted quarterly from start date.

Meet sales goals: Reach annual goal $2 mil revenue.

- COS maximum 20%.

- Less than 5% receivables over sixty days.

- Score 8+ on customer satisfaction surveys.

Promote above-standard performance: Prepare 1> employees for promotion annually.

(Recommendations for performance-related terminations must have documentation of at least two, no more than three Performance Improvement Action Plans detailing counseling sessions for consistent below-standard performance.)

Submit sales reports: On-time receipt and 100% accuracy on all reports.

- Weekly *Sales to Plan Report* due Tues. noon.

- Monthly *Sales Report* due five business days after month end

Performance Expectations for Sales Representative

<u>Responsibilities</u>   <u>Quantity and Quality Performance Expectations</u>

Attendance: Fewer than two late arrivals, early leaves or absences per quarter or fewer than five total per year. Illness or absence requiring additional time should be discussed with your manager or HR.

Attitude: Uphold in the workplace all team members' rights to:

- Be heard.

- Be treated respectfully.

- Express ideas.

Meet sales expectations: (New hire will reach within 90 days.)

- $5,000 wk.

- Avg. sale $650.

- Avg. 8 signed contracts per wk.

- Less than 5% total receivables over sixty days.

- Maintain 8+ customer satisfaction rating.

Submit sales reports: On-time receipt.

- Weekly *Sales to Plan Report* due Monday 10 a.m.

- Monthly *Sales by Industry/Product Report* due two business days after mo. end.

Measure and communicate:

- Know your & overall team goals and status.

- Know your job expectations and status.

- Can define how you are measured.

- Can tie your compensation to expectations.

As the Titletown example illustrates, performance expectations are directly associated with the responsibilities of the job. Clear, simple, meaningful expectations lead to desired results and responsibilities being accomplished. If the company's desired results are increased revenue, profitability, satisfied customers, and a strong and steady workforce, then these simple expectations can help the team achieve them.

Expectations should reflect overall results and critical measurement criteria. Obtain quality coaching assistance to train management on how to think about and write expectations. Avoid laundry lists of micromanagement steps to follow. Only clear, simple, meaningful performance expectations will work. One page per job is normally all that is required.

When adding subjective terms to your list of expectations, it is important to remember that performance expectations apply only to behavior and attitude that is job-related, observable, and measurable. If you need more help regarding preparing performance expectations, please see your manager, HR or coaching professional.

Please select one job you supervise. Make a copy of the *Performance Expectation Sheet* in the last chapter at the end of the book and fill in the responsibilities and performance expectations for that job. Check your completed form with your manager to ensure you are in agreement. Feel free to use the Titletown example to help you.

Once performance expectations are set, review them whenever a change takes place or at least annually to be sure they are in line with reaching overall department and company goals. All other actions necessary to coach your way to success are built upon this foundation, so work at improving your and your team's ability to write clear, concise and meaningful expectations.

With this fundamental piece in place, you are ready to take the next step. There are three management success factors that help bring others forward to meet the demands of innovation and changing expectations. We will focus on those next.

Success Factor 1: Recruit and Hire the Best

Recruiting and hiring is a process of elimination. Many people may apply for a job, but few may be qualified candidates who fit the needs of the job. From those few qualified candidates, usually only one individual is going to be hired. There are four basic steps to help a manager eliminate those who do not match the needs of the job and focus on the few who do. Focusing on only those who match your needs improves hiring results. Better hires means more productive coaching can take place.

Step 1. Prepare - Know what you need.

Step 2. Recruit - Search for candidates who appear to meet your needs.

Step 3. Interview - Make candidates demonstrate they can meet your needs.

Step 4. Hire - Select the candidate who best meets your needs.

The need to hire has some recognizable triggers; most commonly, someone leaves, someone gets promoted or business growth requires additional personnel. Events such as these often leave a void in the day-to-day operation of the business. In our haste to fill a position as quickly as we can, it is easy to skip steps in the process. There are consequences associated with skipping steps and some of the most serious ones are:

- Being unclear about what you are looking for because you did not take the time to assess the "must-have" needs of the job.

- Running a poor ad that tends to draw many resumes, few of which match your needs.

- Believing what you hear rather than what you see by not asking for and observing demonstrations of skills during the interview.

- Hiring someone who does not meet the "must-have" needs of the job, which decreases both your and your new hire's chances for success.

When the four steps are taken, better hiring decisions are made.

Just think what it would be like if you had great candidates waiting in the wings every time you needed to increase or replace staff. Picture no rushing to write up an ad, minimal gaps in work or revenue production, and little impact to customers and other members of the team.

This may not be practical given everything else we have to do in our busy workday. However, by infusing this simple and effective process, we can save valuable time and be well on our way to more successful hiring. Each step represents a specific goal to be reached. If we accomplish each goal along the way, our chances of hiring the right person for the job increase dramatically.

To recruit and hire consistently and effectively, you must accomplish these four steps:

Step 1. Prepare - Know what you need.

Know the responsibilities and performance expectations of the job you are hiring for.

Determine the "must-have" qualifications a candidate needs in order to have the best chance of meeting those expectations.

Step 2. Recruit - Search for candidates who appear to meet your needs.

Determine where to find the best candidates.

Communicate exactly what you want, in the same way, in every place you advertise.

Review resumes and applications to match qualifications and find disqualifiers.

Step 3. Interview - Make candidates demonstrate they can meet your needs.

Utilize job-relevant demonstrations to determine each applicant's ability to meet "must-have" job qualifications.

Step 4. Hire - Select the candidate who best meets your needs.

Once you find the candidate that best demonstrates the ability to meet the needs of the job, check references, including educational background, if a requirement for the position. If all is in good order, happily extend your offer.

Let's look at each in depth.

Qualifications, the first category of needs on the *Recruiting & Hiring Worksheet*, represents the experience and skills any candidate you hire **must** bring to the job to have the best chance of meeting the expectations and being successful.

- If the job you are hiring for has requirements that can be assessed by simply asking and receiving a YES or NO answer, list those first. Examples of these special YES/NO requirements might be:

- For a warehouse position: must be able to lift 50 lbs.

- For a sales rep: must sign a non-compete agreement.

- For a service rep: must be bi-lingual in English and Spanish.

- For a delivery driver: must have a good driving record.

- For a management position: must have a college degree.

Referring to the *Recruiting & Hiring Worksheet* example on the previous page, the Titletown manager must have a sales representative who can demonstrate sales ability. A sales manager spends most of the time training and coaching sales reps. However, this manager wants to start with someone who is accustomed to being a successful salesperson. This makes adapting to the Titletown process much easier and usually means a shorter learning curve. If a candidate does not have applicable sales experience, this person may be difficult to train or require a longer time before she/he is able to reach standard. To meet and exceed revenue goals, this manager would rather hire a more qualified individual capable of obtaining high productivity levels faster. The choice here is to train and coach to fewer, more specific performance areas.

The second category of needs we are concerned with centers on personality traits. This embodies traits and characteristics seen in those people who consistently meet and exceed the expectations of this position. For instance, this manager knows successful sales reps are often people who prefer to learn what customers need and then deliver more, rather than tell customers what they need and deliver that or less.

Notice all needs listed are "must-have" needs. "Must-haves" are basic needs applicants must bring with them to the job in order to be successful. Another way to say this is, YOU ARE NOT GOING TO TRAIN THEM in these needs. You may train them in your company's ways, but they must come with basic knowledge and experience having done these things successfully for someone else.

For those who are hiring entry-level positions, you might think there are no "must-have" needs. Not true. There are always certain skills, experiences or personality traits that the individual must have to be successful on the job, no matter what the job is. An invoicing clerk must have computer and organizational skills, be detail and task-oriented, follow instructions, and may need some alphabetic and numeric skills depending upon your system.

Only listing the "must-haves" helps to ensure you stay focused on the critical needs of the job during the recruiting and hiring process and helps prevent hiring someone who does not bring experience, skills or traits needed to succeed on the job. Remember, the more the candidate brings in "must-have" understanding and experience, the better the chances she/he will, if hired, achieve and exceed job performance expectations. If the person is that good, she/he may even be eligible for promotion in a year or two. What a tribute to the hiring manager.

Make a copy of the *Recruiting & Hiring Worksheet* in the last chapter of the book and fill in the "must-have" needs for the same job you used to complete the *Performance Expectation Sheet* in the last section. Make sure only the "must-have" needs critical to achieving the performance expectations are listed. You are filling in only the first column. The remaining columns will be used during other portions of the recruiting and hiring process. Check your completed form with your manager to ensure you are in agreement. Feel free to use the Titletown example *Recruiting & Hiring Worksheet* to help you.

Legal Considerations:

Each of the four steps of the recruiting and hiring process has specific related legal considerations. Please pay special attention to these pages.

Focus on only the necessary qualifications required to perform the job. Do not write anything besides these necessary qualifications on any job description or *Performance Expectation Sheet*.

Be cautious about arbitrarily setting limits for education or experience. Depending on the job, you may wish to allow some flexibility. You might eliminate excellent candidates who may have a two-year college degree and work experience very complementary to the job you are hiring for if your "must-haves" indicates a four-year college degree and five years of related work experience. The reverse is also true. Restrictions should help, not hinder your ability to hire the best person for the job.

Be cautious about watering down what you know works best. If the clear majority of those successful in the job have certain degrees and/or experience, then the criteria may indeed be appropriate "must-haves."

Needs are specific to the qualifications (education, experience, skills) and personality traits best suited to success on the job. Personal information that has no relationship to meeting the needs of the job would never be listed or even considered. These include marital status, religious affiliation, parental status, gender, etc.

What have you learned so far?

What are the three management success factors?

What are some of the consequences of missing steps in the recruiting and hiring process?

What is the first of the four steps in the recruiting and hiring process?

What are performance expectations?

The first category of needs on the *Recruiting & Hiring Worksheet* is

The second category of needs on the *Recruiting & Hiring Worksheet* embodies the _____ seen in those who consistently meet and exceed the expectations of this position.

Which needs are most important to focus on during the recruiting and hiring process and why?

What are the two most critical things that must be done to accomplish the preparation step in the recruiting and hiring process?

_____

_____

Which of the following should never appear as a need?

    a. Experience

    b. Education

    c. Skill levels

    d. Religious affiliation

What are the four steps of the recruiting and hiring process?

    1._____

    2._____

    3._____

    4._____

(See next page for answers. If you need help, see your manager.)

What have you learned so far? (Answers)

What are the three management success factors?

- Recruit and hire the best people for the job.

- Train and coach everyone to meet the performance expectations of the job, promoting consistently standard or above-standard performers and terminating consistently below-standard performers.

- Conduct performance reviews fairly, positively, and in a timely manner.

What are some consequences of missing steps in the recruiting and hiring process?

- Being unclear about what you are looking for because you did not take the time to assess "must-have" needs of the job.

- Writing a poor ad that draws many resumes, few of which match your needs.

- Believing what you hear rather than what you see by not asking for and observing demonstrations of skills during the interview.

- Hiring someone who does not meet the "must-have" needs of the job, which decreases both your chances for success.

What is the first of the four steps in the recruiting and hiring process?

Prepare

What are performance expectations?

- They state what is expected in a job and how it will be measured.

The first category of needs on the *Recruiting & Hiring Worksheet* is:

Qualifications

The second category of needs embodies <u>personality traits</u> seen in those who consistently meet and exceed the expectations of this position.

Which needs are most important to focus on during the recruiting and hiring process?

<u>All "must-have" needs.</u>

What are the two most critical things that must be done to accomplish the preparation step in the recruiting and hiring process?

- Know the responsibilities/performance expectations of the job you are hiring for.

- Determine the "must-have" qualifications and traits a candidate must bring to the job to have the best chance of meeting those expectations.

Which of the following should never appear as a need:

<u>d. Religious affiliation</u>

What are the four steps of the recruiting and hiring process?

Step 1. Prepare - Know what you need.

Step 2. Recruit - Search for candidates who appear to meet your needs.

Step 3. Interview - Make candidates demonstrate they can meet your needs.

Step 4. Hire - Select the candidate who best meets your needs.

Step 2. Recruit

Search for candidates who appear to meet your needs.

Just ask yourself, "Where do I get most of my good employees?" The answer may be referrals, internal job postings or outside ads. Whatever your answer is, it is important to look for potential candidates from as many sources as possible. You most often need to reach a wide segment of your audience to yield a single hire, so it is best to tap multiple sources. Internet-based search firms usually allow you to tap into their database and search for resumes of people who meet your specific needs. How rich the database is usually determines cost and effectiveness.

Some of the many sources available to you are:

Job Postings

Job Fairs

Networking and Referrals

US Immigration Office

Newspaper Employment Pages

Open Houses

Trade Journal Employment Ads

Campus Recruiting

Recruiting Web Sites

Direct Inquiries

State and Local Unemployment Websites

List all the sources you currently use:

_____

_____

_____

List new sources you will start using:

_____

_____

_____

Now you must prepare one great ad or posting you can broadcast through all sources you decide to use. The message must be the same to ensure consistency in your recruiting and hiring process.

The ad or positing should convey six points to the reader:

1. Position title/ad header.

2. A sentence describing your company and what you are looking for.

3. An outline of some critical job responsibilities.

4. A few bulleted "must-have" qualifications and traits.

5. What your company offers its employees.

6. What action one should take if interested in applying.

Here is a sample Titletown ad used to attract outside sales representatives.

1. Experienced Outside Sales Rep

2. Titletown, a fast-growing local sign company, is seeking an experienced outside sales rep.

3. Rep will develop an existing territory and build existing and new customer relationships based on helping clients grow their businesses through creative use of signage.

4. This position requires:

- strong consultative sales ability

- excellent communication strengths

- positive attitude

- proven track record of sales results

5. We offer excellent products, high 5 figure first-year earning potential, company car, medical, dental, and 401(k) benefits.

6. If you are looking for a true career opportunity and can demonstrate the qualifications we need, please send your resume and cover letter to:

Sales Manager
Titletown Sign Company
123 Main Street
Titletown, USA
Fax: (666) 426-6464   Email: sales@titletown.com

Using the *Performance Expectations* and the *Recruiting & Hiring Worksheet* you have already completed, write up an ad for a job you supervise. Be sure to include all six points.

How PREPARED Are You to RECRUIT?

On a scale of 1 to 10 (10 = highest) rate yourself on how well you do each of the following:

Rating

_____ I recruit and hire the best people for the job because it is one of my managerial responsibilities.

_____ I have a sheet of written performance expectations for each position I supervise (performance expectations are outcomes expected in a job and how they will be measured).

_____ I have a list of the "must-have" needs for each position I supervise.

_____ I am always looking for potential candidates for the jobs I supervise.

_____ I hand to or ask for business cards of people I see who appear to meet some of my needs.

_____ I am always looking for new sources of good people.

_____ When writing an ad to attract good candidates, I check to be sure all six points are covered.

_____ After preparing the ad, I use the same one in all sources I recruit from.

_____ Some of the candidates who contact me are referrals from my current staff.

_____ When writing a new ad/posting, I ask my manager, HR department or other business people I respect for input to ensure I am not discriminating.

_____ **TOTAL** ÷ 10 = _____.   Circle your score below:

1--1.5--2--2.5--3--3.5--4--4.5--5--5.5--6--6.5--7--7.5--8--8.5--9--9.5--10

Not Prepared   Somewhat Prepared   Well Prepared

In this segment of the search phase you are now ready to review resumes to match needs and find disqualifiers. Recruiting and hiring is a process of attracting quality applicants and eliminating those who do not meet the "must-have" needs. The more effective the ad, the more quality responses should be received. Quality versus quantity is the goal. Of all that do come in, we now must eliminate those responses that do not warrant consideration and determine which ones to move forward with.

Both the resume and application must be reviewed, not only to weed out the obvious, but also to determine which applicants are qualified to move on to the next step in the process. The purpose is to continue eliminating candidates by finding disqualifiers. Applicants should fill out the application completely before the interview, even if they have given you a resume, for two reasons:

1.   The application may be a legal requirement in your state.

2.   It is the best means of comparison to the resume, allowing you to check for discrepancies, red flags, and disqualifiers.

There are many things to look for when reviewing the resume and application:

- cover letter specific to position

- appearance/uniqueness/creativity

- spelling, grammar, punctuation

Let's focus on a few particulars.

Can you read it – The care an applicant exhibits when preparing the resume and application may lend insight into how she/he will perform on the job. Overall appearance is one indicator of performance. Also, you might be able to detect the individual's level of written communication skills, if these skills are a requirement for the position. Be careful! There are companies out there making a good living preparing resumes for people. At this stage in the recruiting phase you have no idea who prepared this resume. Don't start jumping to conclusions, one way or another.

What's not there – Something missing is an indicator of an area to explore – not an automatic rejection. For example, a female may have a year gap between jobs. At this stage, again, you don't know why. Was it left open because she was let go from a job for poor performance and does not want to discuss it? Did she re-enter the job market after having a child or taking care of an elderly parent? One may be a problem. The others are not. Again, don't jump to conclusions!

Accomplishments – Specifically, what has the candidate accomplished and was it work-related? Bear in mind that a lack of accomplishments does not necessarily indicate an idle person. Some people may have a tendency to downplay their accomplishments or have difficulty saying positive things about themselves without feeling like they are bragging. Would this present an issue for this job?

What is different about reviewing applications versus resumes? Absolutely nothing. Compare the information on both to check for inconsistencies.

The only additional point regarding an application is *an omission*. In this case, the application is incomplete. Some omissions may be oversights. Or they may be intentional. A critical piece of information on the application is salary history. Individuals fail to complete the salary history for many reasons. Wage history, whether salary, commission or bonus, is critical information for the hiring manager and should be completed before the interview begins. Before moving to the next step in the hiring process, all blanks and omissions must be filled in to your satisfaction.

Do you disqualify someone with adequate experience and qualifications because of frequent job changes? Not necessarily, but it can be an indication of a pattern of behavior. But there's no way to know yet. If you ask for a cover letter and don't get one, do you disqualify? Not necessarily, but it can be an indicator of non-conformance or attention to detail issues.

The hiring manager is responsible for reviewing resumes and ensuring a complete application is provided. This applies even if you use resume reading software.

Now let's go back to the *Recruiting & Hiring Worksheet* introduced in step one of the recruiting and hiring process. This same tool you used to fill in the critical needs of the job can now be used to help keep a clear and consistent focus when reviewing resumes and applications. Compare what is on the resume and application to the list of critical needs on your *Recruiting & Hiring Worksheet*. Do not start making notes, just compare. This often helps to quickly point out disqualifiers. Let's explore an example of locating disqualifiers.

Using the Titletown sales representative worksheet from the previous chapter, the listed needs contain communication skills (listen, speak, write) and professionalism. One resume you see is handwritten and very difficult to read. It contains many misspellings on the words you can make out, and sentence structure is poor. Someone sending in a resume is voluntarily demonstrating for you the "first impression" sample of her/his written communication skills and professionalism. If you have these needs listed on the *Recruiting & Hiring Worksheet*, they must be important to success on the job. So, although the experience *that you could read* on the resume might seem to match, two of your "must-haves" (written communication skills and professionalism) clearly do not.

The most important thing to remember is to be consistent in your expectations. If one category is considered unsatisfactory on one application or resume, then all other applications or resumes with the same or similar information should be considered unsatisfactory.

Legal Considerations:

Treat everyone equally and consistently.

List only the basic "must-have" qualifications.

Avoid language that may discriminate.

All ads should have the same language.

Keep all resumes received for at least one year.

Step 3. Interview

Make candidates demonstrate they can meet your needs.

Conducting a phone screen can quickly eliminate unqualified candidates in the fifteen to twenty minutes it takes to complete it. Except when appropriate to apply in person, all applicants should be called before being brought in for interviews. Remember, this is an elimination process. Interviews take up a lot of your and the candidates' time, so we need to screen out those who should not be brought in.

Some managers feel they do not have time to make a call. You don't have time not to use the telephone as a tool. A few minutes on the phone will save hours in an unproductive interview. Screening eliminates the obvious. You may be able to tell over the phone that an individual does not meet certain criteria for the position. Or, on the other hand, given additional information about the job, the applicant may withdraw. In either case you've saved both parties time and effort.

A phone call allows you to focus on eligible candidates. Start with the best, most promising resumes and have a supply of *Recruiting & Hiring Worksheets* with the job needs listed as you begin making your calls. The worksheet is a simple tool allowing you to rate each applicant's phone screen in a consistent manner. Three days and ten screens later you may not remember what was said by whom.

A very short, informal way of opening up the call is to introduce yourself and say you are calling in response to her/his resume/application for the position. Then ask what the person knows about your company. What you are looking for here is to see if this individual is truly interested in your position or any position. Are they looking for a job with your company or any company?

If someone says she/he has no idea what your company does, or has never heard about your company, does this automatically disqualify her/him? Probably not. But if the person knows something, anything, it may be a plus. It's important to note, depending on the position, the best people may have already screened you. They've done their homework.

On balance, the applicant does most of the talking in these first few minutes. Your job is to ask the right questions and listen. A great question to start with is:

What interests you about this position and why do you feel you are qualified?

Pertinent questions are necessary, of course. Open-ended questions are crucial to get the candidate talking. Listening skills are critical. Answers to good open-ended questions can give you a wealth of information. Most people think what they need to conduct an effective screen is a *long* list of questions. The opposite is true. Lists of questions tend to focus the manager on asking the next question, rather than listening to the response. The manager often ends up concentrating on "What do I ask next?" or "Did I ask that already?"

The phone screen is the best time to determine the applicant's ability to meet any specific requirements your company or you have, so the next questions might be closed ended: "Every employee in this position is required to sign a non-compete agreement. Does that present any problem for you?"

Other examples of specific requirements include:

- job is third shift

- have to work every Saturday

- commission job with draw for first three months

And last but not least, the phone screen is the time to ensure the applicant's earning expectations are in line with what the job pays. This can be the greatest source of annoyance to the applicant and to you because if you wait to broach this critical subject, which is often a clear disqualifier, it has wasted time for both of you. Many people may feel uncomfortable asking about money until later in the process, so they often hold back. One way to ask for this important information is: "For any new job you take, what do you need to be earning in the first year and how does that compare with what you earned last year?"

Remember to ask the same questions to all applicants. If you are not comfortable with some answers, ask for more information right then or make a note and come back to it later. Inside of five to fifteen minutes, you should have gained enough broad-level information to make a decision as to whether you want to invite the candidate in or not. Invite the person in if she/he is that impressive. Very good candidates do not stay in the market that long. Whether you invite a candidate in for an interview or are unsure, immediately after completing a call, use a *Recruiting & Hiring Worksheet* to rate the candidate's ability so far.

Nothing is worse than finding out within the first five minutes of an interview that the applicant has no chance of being successful in the position, and you can't find a professional, courteous way of ending the interview for the next twenty minutes. The phone screen is a great way to avoid this.

What follows is a suggested screen flow format. It is short, simple, and can help you keep on track. Using the same position that you have been practicing with in prior exercises, practice the screen flow with your manager or a peer and see how it works for you.

Screen Flow Example:

This is _____ from (company name). Is (applicant name) there?

Hello, (applicant name). Thank you for sending us your resume. I'd like to learn a little about your interest in our (position title) position. Do you have about fifteen minutes? (If, yes) Tell me (applicant name), what do you know about our company? (Listen). What interests you about this position and why do you feel you are qualified? (Listen and if you need more information, say "Tell me more.")

Every employee in this position is required to (any applicable requirement). Does that present any problem for you? (If response is NO, you can say "good." If the response is yes, just drop to the last paragraph starting with "Thank you.")

Our company is an exciting place to work. What attracts most people is (Tell a few things that attract most to work for your company).

For any position you might accept, what do you need to earn in the first year and how does that compare with what you earned last year? (If applicant states an amount that is far from your range let her/him know average realistic first year's earnings and true growth potential, if any. Your screen should end here if applicant cannot earn what she/he needs or if growth areas are not desirable. Just drop to the last paragraph starting with "Thank you.")

Our next step is to review all applicants we've talked to on the phone. We will then call those we wish to interview. This should occur within the next (number of days/weeks). If you should be one of those we call, how would you feel? (If positive response, "Great.")

Thank you, (name), for taking the time to speak with me. I've enjoyed talking with you.

If applicant starts to ask questions and you have enough time and you feel this is a valid candidate, please respond. If there is not enough time or this is not a valid candidate, just say:

"I would like to take more time to answer your questions but I'm afraid my schedule is pressing. Should we contact you for an interview, we will plan plenty of time to discuss your questions then. Thanks again for speaking with me."

If not comfortable addressing any particular question, be honest:

"I am not comfortable addressing that question at this time. Should we contact you for an interview, we will plan plenty of time to discuss your questions then. Thanks again for speaking with me.

Legal Considerations:

Be sure to avoid asking questions about or discussing:

> Age
> Race
> Sex
> Religion
> National Origin
> Height and Weight
> Arrest Record
> Children
>
> Citizenship
> Discrimination Charges
> Family or Marital Status
> Financial Status

Disabilities
Political Affiliation
Sexual Orientation
Workers' Compensation Claims
Belonging to a Union
Health Issues

Be objective.

Watch what you say over the phone. Be careful of seemingly innocent conversation. The candidate may say something about having a child. A response like "Oh, how many children do you have?" or "You sound older and we need some maturity in the organization" has nothing whatsoever to do with the job and can open you up to all types of legal issues. When a candidate mentions an area you should not discuss, just move on to your next question. Or, if the candidate gets off track and does not fully answer the original question, simply restate it.

Do not address or write down issues of age, marital status, religion, etc. If a candidate tells you something you're not allowed to ask, DO NOT write it down. It has nothing to do with the *Recruiting & Hiring Worksheet* needs or the job.

All questions and notes you jot down must be job related. Regardless of intent, there are no exceptions.

Be consistent with questions.

DO NOT ask or respond to questions about personal information. You can simply say, "I am really interested in discussing more about the job" and move on to your next question.

What did you learn that was new or interesting about the phone screen portion of the interview?

_____

_____

How do you feel about initially calling each applicant? (pros/cons)

_____

_____

Legally, what are considered some of the things you **do not** need to know and should not discuss?

_____

_____

Having read this chapter, what might you change or do differently when you conduct your calls in the future? Why?

_____

_____

When conducting interviews it is most important to stay focused on determining the candidate's ability to meet the "must-have" qualifications of the job.

How do we know someone can do what she/he says? When do we find out? Many managers believe that you can never really know if the person you interview can do the job until she/he is actually doing it. There is strong proof to the contrary. By developing good interviewing skills, we can increase our ability to determine many of the answers to a candidate's ability before we make the decision to hire. One very successful way is to have the candidate focus on showing us what she/he does or has done in similar situations. There is a great way to do this. Ask for demonstrations.

Demonstrations should be tied to your list of "must-have" needs and be relevant to what the person will be doing on the job. If we need a person who has consultative selling skills, and the applicant says she/he can and does sell consultatively, then we should be able to ask that applicant to show us. We want to see how well each person "does" something compared to others interviewed to determine if we should continue keeping her/him as a candidate. Every candidate should be given the same demonstration in order to be consistent and to compare fairly.

Most demonstrations should incorporate multiple needs. Developed skills usually tie a group of thoughts, actions, and personality traits together. Let's look at examples of skill, experience, and personality demonstrations for a few different jobs. As you read these, consider other valuable information you would obtain from your candidate if you use a demonstration. An example for the sales rep demonstration would be insight into how knowledgeable the candidate is about her/his current customers and competitors. As this knowledge is very relevant to success in most sales positions, what a person knows and uses in her/his previous or current job can be a great forecaster of what will be learned and used in future positions.

Interview Demonstration Examples:

1. Position: Sales Representative

"Must-have" Needs:

- Sales experience

- Consultative selling approach:

    - ask questions/learn needs

    - match solutions to needs

- Persistence

Demonstration: Please define your current customer for me. *(Listen intently, as you want to play a prospect.)* Tell me what three things most customers like and three common complaints customers make about your product/service. Who are your top two competitors and what do they offer that is better than what you offer?

I'll play a new prospect you are meeting for the first time. You sell me your product using the sales process you are most comfortable and successful with.

2. Position: Customer Service Representative

"Must-have" Needs:

- Customer service experience

- Communication skills

- Patience

Demonstration: Give me two or three examples of the most common customer service problems you currently respond to. *(Listen intently as you want to play a customer.)* I'm going to play one of your customers with a problem. You help me using the service methods you are most comfortable and successful with.

3. Position: Accounts Payable Clerk

"Must-have" Needs:

- EXCEL spreadsheet experience

- Attention to detail

- Analytical skills

Demonstration: *(Prepare for demonstration by gathering three months' copies of three types of bills that are not business sensitive. Set the PC screen at start-up where the EXCEL icon appears.)* I am going to place you at one of our PCs for about ten minutes and ask you to create, from these sample bills, a new EXCEL spreadsheet to track disbursements for the year. The disbursement categories are (i.e., rent, office supplies, and phone). Ready?

4. Position: Sales Manager

"Must-have" Needs:

- Management skills

- Employee relations sensitivity

- Communication skills

Demonstration: You just got the job as sales manager and this is your first week. A rep comes to your office door and, in an angry voice, points to you and says, "I need to talk to you." Let the candidate take it from there. You play rep demanding more money or you'll walk out right now.

For a second demonstration, play employee who has complained before about a client who keeps making unsavory, sexual comments and nothing has been done.

The "must need" personality traits are not always easy to uncover. A savvy candidate may be able to put on a show to impress you that may not truly reflect who she/he is. Using a highly accurate personality profile tool to assist in the hiring process helps considerably. Along with these profiles, demonstrations become very important in helping you uncover and confirm the applicant can do what she/he claims. A bit more on these profile tools later.

It is important to plan ahead and document all demonstrations you plan to use. Write down the instructions and test them on your manager and a member of your staff to ensure they are clear and concise. You can give the instructions verbally or in writing based on what is most appropriate for the job in question. Just be sure you deliver the instructions the same way all the time. This is to help you be clear and consistent with each candidate. If you explain something two different ways, you may give an advantage to one candidate you did not give to another, flavoring the results you will see and possibly unfairly impacting the decisions you will make later.

When asking candidates to show you what they can do, it is important they comprehend the question and what you expect of them, so answer any questions they have that are related to understanding the assignment. *DO NOT TELL* them how to respond or coach them along. If your "must have" needs are things you will *NOT TEACH TO*, that means the candidate must already know something about how to do what you are asking.

If previous experience is required, it is wise to end your interview by telling the candidate your performance expectations and asking the candidate to tell you how she/he would meet or exceed them. This is a great way to see if, after all the time spent, the applicant has a good grasp of the position and can relate prior experience to answering the question. It also tells you if the candidate understands what performance expectations are and ensures the candidate knows you have them.

Immediately after completing the interview, take out that applicant's *Recruiting & Hiring Worksheet* and rate her/his ability to meet the needs of the job.

Here are a few hints about conducting an interview.

- Plan enough time in the interview to conduct the top two or three critical demonstrations. Each demonstration should average ten minutes or more depending on the depth of the situation and the needs of the job. Use ten minutes as a guide when first starting out.

- Ask open-ended questions. Practice your questions with your manager to ensure they are job related. Ask job-related questions ONLY as there are no other questions that apply in an interview.

- Listen. Listen. Listen. Make a note if you need to come back to something and do not stop listening. Ask for more information if a response is insufficient and do not stop listening.

- Politely, stop the candidate if the conversation is getting off track and bring the candidate back to the job-related issue you need to discuss. This is not a rude thing to do. It is a necessary thing to do.

- If you make a note, make it a simple job-related word or phrase that will jog your memory later to ask about it. Using a sticky note works great for this. No long paragraphs or non-job-related words ever apply. Check off each item on the sticky note when you are satisfied it has been addressed. Once you have rated the applicant on the *Recruiting & Hiring Worksheet*, you no longer need to keep the notes.

- Immediately after the interview, rate the candidate on the *Recruiting & Hiring Worksheet*. If you wait, you may not remember everything to help you rate accurately.

- When you find the person who best meets the needs of the job, you are ready to hire.

If you have interviewed three or more candidates and no one is meeting the needs, and you are tempted to lower your expectations because you are getting nervous, think again. Hiring someone who does not have the qualifications and personality traits required to be successful in the job, knowing you do not have time or are not in a position to train them in what they lack, dramatically increases the chances the person will not succeed. Is the high risk worth it? No, it is not.

So instead of making this big mistake, check a few things before proceeding to interview more candidates:

- Is there any common thread that each applicant seems to be falling short in?

- Are my demonstrations clear and easily understood?

- How could I change my phone screen to prevent wasting valuable interview time?

- Could I add a demonstration to my phone screen to identify better-qualified candidates?

Using the same position you supervise that you have been practicing with in prior exercises, please create demonstrations you would use during the interview. See how many of your "must-have" needs you can uncover in each.

Do this exercise now while the information is fresh and to gain practice.

If unsure at any time on how to proceed, request coaching assistance from your manager, HR or your professional coach if you have one.

Step 4. Hire

Select the candidate who best meets your needs.

Check References

Professional reference checks can be extremely helpful. A sample reference checking form is on the next page. This is a tool to help the hiring manager gather consistent information from reference sources. Beyond confirmation of employment dates, positions, and wages, information is getting harder and harder to get. The higher up professionally one is in her/his career, the easier it may be to obtain references that will talk to you candidly. Get as many as you can from as many sources as you can.

If the position you are hiring for is a management position, ask for three people the candidate reported to, three people who were peers on the management team, and three people who reported to the candidate. Former employees may shed insight that is very different than the former managers' observations.

Personal references are the least reliable since people are not likely to give a name as a reference if they aren't sure that person will say good things. They can, however, provide some valuable information if you present work-related, typical situations and ask how the candidate would handle them.

If a particular education level or degree is a requirement for the job, contact the registrar's office at the school listed on the application where the candidate obtained the degree. Check for accuracy and dates. The candidate should be able to provide the phone number, address or e-mail address of the school. If the candidate does not have it handy, she/he can certainly e-mail it to you.

Once the reference checks are completed and satisfactory, you are ready to offer the position.

Offer the Job

Calling the applicant to extend the offer is a wonderful moment. Do not waste time doing this, as highly qualified people are hard to find and someone else may get to them first. If it is Friday afternoon or before a holiday, do not wait. If the candidate is excited about the opportunity your company presents, she/he wants to hear from you. Your generosity with your time and effort to reach them with this important news says a lot to the prospective employee about you as a boss.

SAMPLE **Reference Check**

Applicant _____ Position/Dept. _____

Employer _____ Telephone no. _____

Contact _____ Title _____

Reference check conducted by _____ Date _____

Dates of employment from _____ to _____

Position title when started/when left company? _____ _____

Starting salary? _____ Ending salary?_____ Commission/Bonus?_____

Eligible for rehire? __ Yes __No

Reason for leaving _____

How would you rate her/him on the following: (List each "must-have" need and ask to rate 1-10, 10 = highest.)

How did she/he get along with:

     Co-workers? _____

     Customers/Clients? _____

     Managers? _____

Times a month absent from work? Late? Left early?

Amount of supervision required?

Can you give me a name of another person who can provide a reference?

__Yes __ No If yes: Name _____

Position _____ Telephone no. _____

This candidate:

__ Meets requirements __ Does not meet requirements __ Exceeds Requirements

It is not a good idea to leave the offer on voice mail or e-mail. Leave a message that you very much would like to speak to her/him as soon as possible and to call you, maybe even leaving your personal number if over a weekend. Then make the offer directly. Talk to the person, congratulate the person, confirm the earnings plan, set a start date, and send a confirming letter.

If the candidate declines the offer, be gracious and ask the reason. Always be professional, sincere, and positive. Anything can happen and you should ask the person to call you if she/he has a change of heart or is interested in reconsidering the position in the future. There is no guarantee a position will be available but you are leaving the door open. The note on which you leave the person is critical. Often, these people call you back at a later date to see if opportunities exist or refer others to you who are qualified candidates. After all you went through to find the right candidate, she/he should be held in high regard.

There is an example on the next page of a recommended letter to send to the candidate you elect to hire. Usually you call to place the offer directly and then may choose to send the letter as a follow-up affirming the offer. Your HR department may have letters available or can help draft a letter using appropriate language. Double-check the information you insert for accuracy. You would never want to mislead someone or start on the wrong foot.

After the offer letter, you will find an example of a letter to send to those you *do not* elect to hire. It is recommended that you send letters to those you have brought in for interviews. It is not necessary to send letters to those you telephone screen or those who sent you a resume or filled out an application.

There is certain information that, either by company policy or law, must be retained for at least one year. Check with your HR or state employment office.

Offer (Example Only)

(To be sent to the individual to confirm an employment offer. If you have access to an HR department, it's always best to check employment forms before using them, including form letters.)

Date

Applicant

Address

City, State Zip

Dear _____:

We are pleased you have accepted the position of _____ .
This letter confirms your acceptance and is not a contract.

(If appropriate) Your starting salary will be_____,
and commission (or bonus structure) is payable as
follows:_____.

We look forward to your joining our company on (date) at ___(time) a.m.
Please come to (HR/my office/other and ask for (me/other). If there is
anything I can do to help you before you arrive, please do not hesitate to
contact me.

Sincerely,

Hiring Manager

"Thank you for interviewing." (Example Only)

(When hire has been made, this letter would be sent to all others who interviewed. If you have access to an HR department, it's always best to check employment forms with them before using, including form letters.)

Date

Applicant

Address

City, State Zip

Dear Applicant:

The position you interviewed for has been filled. We appreciate your application for employment and the time you spent in the interview process and wish you success in your job search.

Thank you for your interest in our company.

Sincerely,

Hiring Manager

Legal Considerations:

Watch for many legal pitfalls in the recruiting and hiring process.

If you think a question or action is inappropriate, it probably is. Use your good judgment.

Remain consistent, using only work-related questions, demonstrations, and appropriate letters.

Can you question an applicant on the following: Yes or No

_____ Age

_____ Religion

_____ Arrests

_____ Sick days

_____ Medications

_____ Use of alcohol

_____ Work-related injury

_____ Rent or own a home

_____ Union status

_____ Place of birth

_____ Children

_____ Spouse

_____ Physical impairments

_____ Drug or alcohol addiction

_____ Bankruptcy

_____ Stress

_____ Marital status

All of these should NOT be asked or inquired about.

When to Hire – When to Promote

Promoting people is a big responsibility. Promotions can occur for many reasons, all of which should relate to performance. To ensure promotions meet the *consistency, fairness, and caring* test, it is usually wise to assess the needs of the job to be filled first.

All jobs have needs or specific qualifications and personality traits that, if met, ensure basic responsibilities can be carried out adequately. For example, a sales representative must be able to demonstrate sales ability that relies on listening, speaking, and writing skills, and demonstrate *proactive* problem-solving skills to qualify for the job. A customer service representative must be able to demonstrate listening, speaking, and writing skills, and demonstrate very keen *reactive* problem-solving skills to successfully perform in that job. The sales rep normally must be adept at building long-term customer relationships, uncovering customer challenges and problems, and creatively solving them. The customer service rep rarely speaks to the same customer more than a few times and usually the conversations are with people who are upset or who have problems that need to be solved immediately. Both jobs involve communication and problem solving yet the qualifications and personality traits required to be successful in each job can be quite different.

The manager must focus on what a person needs to bring to the job in order to meet the job expectations. Whether hiring a new person or promoting an existing member of the team, it is important to use the same needs assessment of that job to measure "best fit." After all, an important part of our role as manager is to ensure we do all we can to set the stage for success.

The qualifications and personality traits needed to be successful in the job do not change just because we want to promote someone and that position happens to be open. Here is the key…*always start with knowing the needs of the job. Then match every candidate to those needs to find the "best fit."* The person who gets the job should be the person who best matches the needs of the job. When we promote someone because we like that person or because a position has been open too long and we are under pressure to fill it, we may be setting that employee up to fail. Remember, we succeed if our people succeed.

Consider the differences you face when promoting someone into a job, versus hiring someone from the outside. Existing employees who are interested in moving up in the organization should be aware of the needs of any position they have their sights set on. The manager should be very aware of promotion opportunities, within their department and beyond, that are best suited to the skill set and growth patterns of their various team members. In either case, it is your responsibility as a manager to recognize and acknowledge each team member's need to grow and help prepare them for that next step. There is no greater measure of a manager's ability than to have a track record for hiring and developing good people who excel and grow, preferably but not necessarily, within your organization.

Promoting people on your team is all about preparing those who are performing consistently at or above standard to meet the needs of the job they are next best suited for. Explore this responsibility by reading scenarios 1 and 2 below and answering the questions that follow.

Scenario 1: Jane has been a part-time service rep on Harry's sales team for six months now. She has consistently performed above standard in preparing orders accurately and on time and has often prevented customers from discontinuing service. She has even, on a number of occasions, up-sold the customer because Jane really believes the product works for the customer. Harry is frantically trying to hire two sales reps because he has two territories that have been open for a while. Jane is very interested in becoming a full-time sales rep and has been trying for a few months now to get time with Harry to talk about her goals. Her performance review was due back in April and it is June. Harry keeps telling her he will get to it, but he hasn't yet. He's rarely in the office because he's spending most of his time covering open territories. So trying to get together has been a real problem. Harry feels Jane is only a part-time employee and so it's no big deal. Jane has left notes for Harry explaining how she wants to be considered for an open position, but she hasn't heard anything yet and feels very frustrated. Harry prefers to hire people he does not need to train. He sends them to the company training and believes that is enough. He has his hands full just trying to run open territories because he is always down a few reps. Harry feels keeping a presence in open territories is one of the most important parts of his job, so he makes sure he is out there doing it.

Scenario 2: Jane has been a part-time service rep on Harry's sales team for six months now. She has consistently performed above standard in preparing orders accurately and on time and has often prevented customers from discontinuing service. She has even, on a number of occasions, up-sold the customer because Jane really believes the product works for the customer. Harry is considering promoting Jane to full-time sales rep. During her performance review in April, Jane stated that one of her goals was to become a full-time sales representative within the next year, so Harry knows she wants the position. As part of Jane's development action plan, Harry had given Jane the sales rep job description and a *Performance Expectation Sheet* that states all the qualifications and personality traits that someone must have to be considered for the job. He asked Jane to meet with him when she was prepared to tell and show him how well she matched up to those needs. Jane set that as a goal to be accomplished within the next thirty days. Two weeks later, Jane asks to meet with Harry because she is ready. Jane is excited about sales and demonstrates for Harry that she certainly meets the majority of needs but has no formal training in a sales process. Harry agrees with her and explains that he would like to work together toward her attending the company's sales training program within the next ninety days. She will be given some very specific sales tasks to help her build her selling skills. They work out the hours needed and agree to begin training and coaching next week.

Analyzing the situation:

1. What are the differences in Harry's priorities between each scenario?

_____

_____

2. Based on the needs of the job, do you think Jane is promotable right now? Why?

_____

_____

3. What would you have done differently if you were the manager in this situation?

_____

_____

For scenario 1, what do you predict will happen in the next six months?

_____

_____

For scenario 2, what do you predict will happen in the next six months?

_____

_____

There are various types of promotions managers can make available to their team members. Much depends on the capabilities and desires of the individual and your department or company needs at the time.

If a consistent, good performer desires to take on more responsibility or learn more than her/his current job offers, consider a **lateral** promotion. Lateral promotions allow a good performer to move into and learn another skill area in order to become more valuable to the organization. Once this individual has mastered the new skill, a pay increase may follow because she/

he is now more versatile, able to cover for or help out in more areas, hence is more valuable to the organization.

If a consistent good performer demonstrates a natural ability to help people on the team, the promotion offered might be a **trainer** role. Along with the current job this person is doing, when a new employee is hired, this individual will play a major role in training the new hire in the skills needed to consistently meet the expectations of the job. As a "trainer," this person would warrant an increase if she/he could demonstrate that the majority of trainees reach expectations in the normal time allotted.

Becoming a **trainer/coach** is a way for the successful trainer to increase earnings and gain additional management skills. Here, an increase or promotion may be earned by demonstrating first, that trainees reach expectations in the normal time allotted, and second, that they also hold consistent standard performance over a reasonable time period after training concludes.

These are a few great ways to groom a person for **management**. You have paved the way for building training, coaching, measuring, and communicating experience, all of which are "must-have" needs for any manager.

1. What types of promotions do you currently have available to encourage growth?

_____

_____

2. Talk to your manager and other managers and list at least three new promotion options you might consider that apply to your team.

_____

_____

_____

Most of us have experienced the traditional "up the ladder" promotion. This is where you learned and performed a skill or group of skills very well and you were promoted to supervise others who did that same skill or group of skills. The theory is you will somehow impart your exceptional ability and knowledge to your team.

The potential lack of understanding or preparedness associated with performing management skills (training, coaching, measuring, and communicating) often has no bearing on whether you get the promotion or not. The truth is, we generally place very little emphasis on a frontline manager's ability to hire, train, coach, measure, and communicate to help a team improve. It seems to become an issue only when trouble signs arise like productivity decreases, quality drops off, customers complain more, department morale becomes noticeably poor, or turnover goes up, just to name a few.

The good news is, these end results can be avoided. First, it helps to recognize the importance and needs of the management position and the often negative impacts of promoting the wrong or unprepared person into that position. Second, promote or hire only the best-qualified person for the job who can best hire, train, coach, measure, and communicate. These people are better able to pick up on and deal with issues like absenteeism, productivity decreases and morale problems, coach to improve performance and consequently get the team back on track to reaching its goals.

It's not very difficult to set up a system to prepare to grow and promote people into positions they are qualified for, but for some reason we just don't take the time to do it. The easiest way to prepare people who are aspiring to be managers is to create opportunities for them to practice and demonstrate they can meet the "must-have" needs of that next job. You should be preparing them for the basic management responsibilities before considering them for that type of promotion. Just think of what it would mean to have one or two people on your team who were adept at training and coaching.

It could be as simple as setting up progressive promotion opportunities like trainer and trainer/coach to give them an opportunity to learn and practice. You can use a management profile tool to help determine personality tendencies, in order to determine the best fit for the position. The candidate might be required to complete an in-depth management training program and pass specific, consistent tests and demonstrations before becoming eligible or assuming the position.

A current employee may be selected based on such factors as past performance, experience and knowledge, and an assessment of apparent ability to perform in the new job. Fill every position with the best-qualified and best-suited candidate.

Management's job is to set reasonable expectations, train and coach to those expectations, and measure and communicate along the way to reaching them.

We succeed if our people succeed.

How PREPARED Are You to PROMOTE?

On a scale of 1 to 10 (10 = highest) rate yourself on how well you do each of the following:

Rating

_____ Promotions can occur for many reasons, but I am careful to ensure all promotions I give are performance related, not because the person I promote is my friend or because I just need to fill an opening quickly.

_____ To ensure promotions meet the consistency, fairness, and caring test, I always assess the needs of the job to be filled first and then match the best qualified person to it.

_____ Whether hiring a new person or promoting an existing member of the team into a job, I use the same needs assessment of that job to measure against.

_____ I do not change the requirements, qualifications, and personality traits needed to be successful in the job just because that position happens to be open and I want to promote someone into it quickly.

_____ I make sure employees interested in moving up in the organization are aware of the needs of any position they have their sights set on.

_____ I make sure I am very aware of promotion opportunities, within my department and beyond, that are best suited to the skill set and growth patterns of my team members.

_____ I am very good at recognizing and acknowledging the need to grow in my people and help prepare those whose performance warrants taking that next step.

_____ I have a great track record for hiring and developing good people who excel and grow in the organization.

_____ Various types of promotions are available within my department, depending on the capabilities and desires of the individual looking to be promoted and my department needs at the time.

_____ I enjoy developing people into potential managers and providing lots of opportunity to practice training, coaching, measuring, and communicating so they are prepared when an opportunity arises.

_____ **TOTAL** ÷ 10 = _____.   Circle your score:

1--1.5--2--2.5--3--3.5--4--4.5--5--5.5--6--6.5--7--7.5--8--8.5--9--9.5--10

Not Prepared   Somewhat Prepared   Well Prepared

A Word about Terminations

When an employee's performance is consistently below expectations or a team member continues to pay no attention to rules and disciplinary action, when an offense is repeated, or misconduct is serious enough for discharge on the first offense, decisive action must be taken.

It is your responsibility to consistently hire, train, coach, measure, and communicate to do all you can to assist all employees with bringing performance up to standard and ensure rules and policies are adhered to. When behavior does not improve in any of these areas, there should be no surprise when we consistently ask below-standard employees to leave the team. If we are very good as managers about setting and communicating expectations of performance, we are less likely to let poor performance go unnoticed.

If you are consistent in these practices, what message does this send to your team? You care that each person and the team reach goals; you are fair because you expect everyone on the team to at least reach and consistently perform to expectations and behave in accordance with your company's rules and policies; and you take necessary, sometimes difficult steps to ensure rules and policies are adhered to and performance goals are met.

Good managers handle these situations with consistency, fairness, and caring. These good managers usually attract good people to work on their team, because most people like working in successful, positive environments where they know what is expected of them. And it takes the whole team meeting and exceeding expectations and adhering to rules and policies to create a successful and positive work environment.

Few managers like letting people go. Terminating an employee is often a very difficult and emotional challenge for any manager, regardless of how long we have held that position. As with promoting people, when we terminate someone, we feel the impact we can have on our employees. Management is serious business and the responsibilities should not be taken lightly.

Managers do have the power to make this difficult responsibility less difficult for all involved. That power comes from ensuring termination is never a surprise. We can do so much to help by doing a few things in a caring, fair, and consistent manner. Those things are:

- Setting and consistently managing to reasonable, measurable, and achievable expectations of performance while stating and enforcing the consequences of below-standard performance to the entire team.

- Being consistently diligent about training, coaching, measuring, while communicating frequently and honestly the status of each team member's performance to the expectations.

- Documenting performance issues when they happen, both positive and negative and using action plans to help make documentation easier and more consistent. (Refer to the chapter on Planning for Improvement for more information on action plans.)

- Ensuring you and your employees understand your company policies and procedures and being consistent and diligent about enforcing them.

Management's job is to set reasonable expectations, train and coach to those expectations, and measure and communicate along the way to reaching them.

We succeed if our people succeed.

Planning for Improvement

By continuously working the four steps of recruiting and hiring you increase your opportunity to hire better-qualified people. Hiring people who meet or exceed the needs of the job can help you:

> **Reach goals (more likely to succeed)**
>
> **Save time (easier to train and coach)**
>
> **Save money (hire less staff to compensate for poor performers)**

As you work through each step of the process, refer to this book to help remind you of important tips and tools to use. Ask your manager for assistance at any time. Determine what you would like to improve on. Set goals for yourself and work to improve your ability to recruit and hire the best people for the job. In the forms section at the end of the book is a blank *Performance Improvement Action Plan*. Copy and complete one to help you plan and accomplish these improvements. Goals, like any performance expectation, must be simple, easy to understand, achievable, measurable, and set in a reasonable time frame to be accomplished.

In a coaching environment, you will be asked to prepare and discuss your plan with your manager and together determine coaching or additional training assistance needed on specific areas you are working to improve. As part of your training/coaching plan, role-playing with your manager, HR and with your peers is extremely helpful, giving you insight into approaches you may find useful.

As you work your action plan, consider its value to you. If an action plan can help you focus on improvement in your job, then it can help each member of your team do the same for her/his job. Everyone on your team should know how to complete an action plan and should know you will be looking forward to coaching each of them to help reach the job expectations and goals she/he has set. The ability to reach and exceed your department goals is dependent upon how good your people do their job.

Success Factor 2: Train and Coach to Meet Job Performance Expectations

There are two critical pieces to the puzzle of how to improve performance:

- **Training** provides guided learning of information and practice of skills needed to do a job.

- **Coaching** provides monitoring, guidance, and direction to ensure information and skills required to do the job are implemented properly in order to meet performance expectations.

Scenario 1: Most of us have experienced starting a new job, learning new skills in training, and thinking during training, "Wow, this is easy! The trainer tells me I'm doing great! I can't wait to start using what I just learned." When we go back to the job, our manager asks, "How did you do in training?" and we say, "Great." The manager smiles and says, "We've been waiting for you to get out of training because we are all real busy so we need you to go out there and do what you were taught right away. I know you can do it. Now go out there and do a great job!" We are feeling terrific, head out to do our job using the new skills we just learned and, in very little time, find ourselves saying, "This is weird. I did the task great in training. But here I am on the job and I'm having trouble doing even step 1 right. What's wrong with me?" Now one of two things will usually happen. We keep at it, get frustrated, and soon, because most human beings do not like feeling uncomfortable, we find a way to do the job that feels comfortable and say to ourselves, "So it isn't exactly what I was taught in training, but it works for me." Or, we keep at it, get frustrated, and soon, because most human beings do not like feeling uncomfortable and are very resourceful, we quit and go work somewhere else.

Why does this happen? Not a big mystery if you understand the difference between training and coaching. Let's change the scenario a little and see if you can tell the difference.

Scenario 2: Most of us have experienced starting a new job, learning new skills in training, and thinking during training, "Wow, this is easy! The trainer tells me I'm doing great! I can't wait to start using what I just learned." When the training ends, there is a message from the manager saying, "Please come to my office. I am interested in discussing your training and the next steps we will take in your continued learning process." You think as you walk to the manager's office that this is special and wonder if everyone gets this attention. The manager smiles and says, "I spoke with your trainer who said you did very well. I am so pleased and proud of you. I am interested in what new skills you felt most comfortable with as well as which ones you felt least comfortable with." Together, you and your manager spend the next twenty minutes discussing the training in detail, all the while thinking, "My manager really knows what I was trained in and is genuinely interested in how I did. Nice." Then the manager explains how together both of you are going to set up a *Performance Improvement Action Plan*. The manager explains that this will help you implement all the good things you have learned step by step, little by little, so you can have the best opportunity to be successful in your job. After all, learning a lot of new information and skills during training sets a great foundation, but taking all that new information and putting it into practice on the job can get a little confusing and frustrating. So you spend the next ten minutes working with your manager on this *Performance Improvement Action Plan* to help you perfect your use of steps 1 and 2 *only* over the next two weeks. The manager hands you a sheet with performance expectations on it and explains that this is the performance expected of everyone doing the same job within ninety days of hire and how *Performance Improvement Action Plan*s are intended to help us get there. You remember seeing this same information during your interview. You're thinking, "Expectations are no joke; however, by working the *Performance Improvement Action Plan* with my manager I have the best chance of getting there. I know I can do this."

What differences do you see between scenarios 1 and 2?

_____

_____

_____

If you have ever experienced something similar to scenario 1, what was the outcome?

_____

_____

_____

If you have ever experienced something similar to scenario 2, what was the outcome?

_____

_____

_____

Have you ever worked in a place where everyone doing the same job knew exactly what the performance expectations were? *(Performance expectations state what is expected in a job and how it will be measured.)* Yes_____ No_____

Training provides guided learning of information and practice of skills needed to do a job. **Coaching** provides guidance and direction to ensure information and skills required to do the job are implemented properly in order to meet performance expectations. Successful training and coaching rely heavily on knowing what the performance expectations are and focus on applying all learning, practice, implementation, and development to achieving those expectations.

What have you learned so far?

What are the three management success factors?

1. _____

2. _____

3. _____

What is the difference between training and coaching?

Training _____

Coaching _____

What two outcomes usually occur when someone is not coached after training?

_____

or

_____

Successful training and coaching rely heavily on knowing what the _____

_____ are and applying all skill learning,

practice, implementation, and development to achieving them.

What are performance expectations? _____

_____

_____

List two of the most serious consequences of accepting consistently below-standard performance:

a. _____   b. _____

Expectations that are usually tied to some numeric measurement like how much, how many, how often are considered _____ expectations.

Expectations that relate to specific criteria or parameters like how good, how efficient, how flexible are considered _____ expectations.

Performance expectations must:

    a.   Be clear
    b.   Be simple to communicate
    c.   Be measurable
    d.   Lead to desired results
    e.   All of the above

Whose responsibility is it to train and coach? _____

Check your answers on the next page.

What have you learned so far? (Answers)

What are the three management success factors?

1. Recruit and hire the best people for the job.

2. Train and coach everyone to meet the performance expectations of the job.

3. Conduct performance reviews fairly, positively, and in a timely manner.

What is the difference between training and coaching?

Training provides guided learning of information and practice of skills needed to do a job. **Coaching** provides monitoring, guidance, and direction to ensure information and skills required to do the job are implemented properly in order to meet performance expectations.

What two outcomes usually occur when someone is not coached after training?

We find a way to do the job that feels comfortable even if it isn't what was taught. OR we quit and go work somewhere else.

Successful training and coaching rely heavily on knowing what the *performance_expectations* are and apply all skill learning, practice, implementation, and development to achieving them.

What are performance expectations? *State what is expected in a job and how it will be measured.*

List two of the most serious consequences of accepting consistently below-standard performance:

a. Not reach goal   b. Increase expenses

Expectations that are usually tied to some numeric measurement like how much, how many, how often are considered *quantity* expectations.

Expectations that relate to specific criteria or parameters like how good, how efficient, how flexible are considered *quality* expectations.

Performance expectations must be: <u>e. **All of the above**</u>

a. Be clear
b. Be simple to communicate
c. Be measurable
d. Lead to desired results
e. All of the above

Whose responsibility is it to train and coach? <u>The manager's.</u>

Training

Training provides guided learning of information and practice of skills needed to do a job. It is a valuable tool in any business. Whether you do the training yourself, delegate it to a member of your team or the training department, or send staff to outside programs, it is precious time and should be weighted very heavily in the contribution it can make to the development of your employees and your business.

Types of Training

Companies who have large numbers of employees all doing the same job (management, sales, customer service, office administration, etc.) can benefit greatly from having a training department. The benefit comes when one training program can be designed and delivered to many people efficiently and on a continuing basis. Economies of scale are reached when many participants attend the same program over time. The consistency in information, skill level, process used, and language associated with that job become ingrained into the fabric of the entire organization and can support and help to facilitate quick and efficient changes in the job as the business changes.

For smaller segments of a company's population, there are other ways to train that may be much more cost effective and easier to implement, (i.e. on-the-job, outside classes, shelf programs).

In deciding what training to provide to your employees, consider these few questions:

1. What do you expect the trainee to be able to do upon completion of training?

2. How much time are you willing to allot to achieving those results?

3. How much money are you willing to spend to achieve those results?

Regardless of what type of training is provided, the manager's expectations (number 1 above) are most critical. No other questions can be answered or dealt with until you know what you want the training to accomplish. Some jobs, for instance, can tolerate only a very small margin for error, so the expectation must account for that. Other issues to consider are: type of instruction (hands-on, simulation, computer aided/software, classroom), quality of trainer, quality and quantity of material and equipment to be used during training, size of group.

Sending employees to outside programs or using off-the-shelf books or computer-aided learning tools is fine as long as you are sure the objectives of that program meet your objectives for your trainee.

Most managers provide on-the-job training to their staff. Even after an employee attends a professional inside or outside training program, the manager often finds the employee has not thoroughly learned all skills and will likely need in-depth training on some of the skills again. Given that adults learn best by doing, on-the-job training can be a great practical method. When training is completed, measure results (performance vs. expectations) and continue training as needed.

It is the responsibility of the manager to provide training for her/his team members in the information, skills, and processes needed to do the job and that includes learning to do an old job in a new way. A terrific training department, like any training resource, may or may not provide the specific training for every job in the company or provide it exactly when you need a particular employee to receive it. However, formal, professional inside or outside training is a great tool for you as a manager to take advantage of, as it can set a foundation for you and your employees to build on.

There are very few companies that provide "train until learned" programs where the participant graduates and is returned to you only when she/he can perform specified skills and meet very specific expectations. A pilot must train and pass stringent simulations prior to doing the job, but this is unusual. Most training programs are "time limited." This means the training is focused on helping the majority of the participants learn the information, skills, and process basics in the time allotted. Keep close communication with your company trainer to learn where your participant's skills are strong and where more training should be focused when the formal "time limited" training ends.

Ultimately, the manager is responsible for training each member of the team and most often, is the one providing on-the-job training. Keep in mind, training provides guided learning of information and practice of skills needed to do a specific job, and most people learn by doing. On-the-job training should involve clear, easy-to-follow instruction with guided practice, to ensure the new information is understood and the skill/task is being done as needed on the job. Obviously, one's performance during training may not be as fast or as smooth as that of an employee who has been doing the task for three months.

Training someone in the skills/tasks of a job takes a 1-2-3 approach. First, the trainee must *recognize results expected* of doing the skill/task correctly. The trainee must know what to look for as a result of the task being done right. Second, when observing the task being performed, the trainee must be able to *identify critical steps* performed correctly and in proper sequence. And third, a trainee must *demonstrate performance* of the critical skills/tasks correctly and in proper sequence....with consistency.

1-2-3 training means the trainee can:

1. Recognize results expected when the skill/task is done correctly.

2. Identify critical steps of the task performed correctly and in proper sequence.

3. Demonstrate critical skills/task performed correctly and in proper sequence.

Each step needs to be accomplished before moving on to the next.

To ensure #1 is met, we need a way for the trainee to show us that she/he can recognize the results expected when the task is done correctly. There is usually something that occurs immediately after completing the task that tells you it was done right, i.e., the computer screen changes to another specific screen, the machine shuts down, the report elements total correctly, etc. Ask the trainee to watch you complete the task step by step, calling out the number of each step as you go. As you complete the last step, point out what immediately happens that shows it was done correctly. Ask the trainee to describe the result in detail and when this result should be expected to occur. If the trainee answers correctly, tell her/him to make a written note of the results to better remember what to look for later.

To ensure #2 is met the trainee must observe the task performed in sequence and accurately at least three times. *After* observing at least three correct demonstrations of the task, give the trainee a sheet with the steps for how to complete the task, showing the exact same correct process of completing the task in written or diagram form. The expected result of proper completion of the task should always be shown at the end of the last step as well. You will want to create your written training steps or simple flowchart and test it with someone familiar with the job to ensure it covers all elements in the simplest order needed to train a person in the *basics* of getting the job done. Also, test it with someone unfamiliar with the job to ensure it is clear to read, easy to follow, and works. Mark places where unusual or difficult things can occur and indicate you want the trainee to stop and ask a teammate before moving on.

Have the trainee observe you complete the steps correctly. Hand them the steps, discussing them as you proceed. Now have the trainee observe you again, but this time she/he must follow closely to try to catch you making any mistakes in the steps. If the trainee sees a mistake she/he should say "STOP" right away and tell you what the mistake is. Do it correctly the first time. Now do a second demonstration adding in only one or two of the *most common* mistakes that occur when completing this task. When the expected positive end result does not happen or the error has stopped the process, or the trainee says "STOP," ask the trainee to tell you what went wrong. Every time the trainee says, "STOP" and identifies the error correctly, give her/him a reward (stickers that say "Genius" or congratulate them enthusiastically) and ask the trainee to write down the error she/he identified. Having a list of the "Top Five Errors" can help the trainee remember later what they are and how to avoid them.

Repeat the demonstrations until the following two things happen:

1. You have included, one or two at a time, all of the top five *most common* mistakes that occur when performing this task.

2. The trainee consistently recognizes all of the steps and common mistakes.

To ensure #3 is met, the employee is now asked to demonstrate the task performed. The trainee should use the **STEPS** sheet or flowchart to help move along and she/he should ask you any questions while progressing. The trainee needs to know you will be happy to help. Every time the trainee completes the task and gets to that expected correct end result, she/he knows that means the job was done right. Every time this happens give the trainee a small reward (i.e., genius sticker, package of Post-it notes, or an enthusiastic "congratulations"). The objective here is for the trainee to perform the task *correctly* and in proper sequence three or more times). Adding appropriate little rewards makes it fun and, believe it or not, improves chances of success. Using appropriate rewards when training a manager sends a clear message to do the same when that manager is training others.

DO NOT interrupt or stop a trainee working through the steps of the task (unless some terrible or irreversible thing will happen as a result of the incorrect action). If she/he makes a mistake, say nothing, and allow the trainee to continue. Remember she/he can ask you questions any time and you will help, but if the trainee does not ask, let her/him continue. You might need to remind the person that you will answer any questions. Not saying anything when a mistake occurs is the hardest part of training because we want to jump in and "rescue" the trainee from making that mistake. But most people learn from their mistakes and improve. People who do not learn from their mistakes have difficulty growing and improving in that job. We need to know that every employee can learn from mistakes because those that can, most likely, will reach standard performance expectations in the time allotted and continue to grow.

Each time the task is completed *incorrectly* and the expected result does not happen or an error has stopped the process, ask the trainee to go back over the task elements completed to check her/his work and find the error. If trainees learn to correct their own errors, they will learn and improve more quickly. Avoid teaching people to come to you every time something happens. Train them to solve most problems themselves.

A great way to tie performance expectations to training is to hand the trainee a copy of the job performance expectations you provided when you hired the person. Have her/him describe for you any expectations that relate to the task being trained on. Listen closely and correct understanding along the way. Once the trainee can describe the correlation correctly, ask her/him to write down the expectations that apply. This will tell you what the trainee does or does not understand about the expectations and gives the trainee an opportunity to read, write, and discuss each with you. You are then correcting any performance expectation misunderstandings right up front associated with the task you are training on. Incorporate different methods (reading, writing, interaction, talking) to reinforce learning. After training is accomplished, trainees should be evaluated on how well they did in each task and what areas they need to work on. Together, trainee and trainer should place this information on a *Performance Improvement Action Plan.*

When you are the trainer, using this simple 1-2-3 method can go a long way to making on-the-job training the best it can be. Measure the effectiveness of your training by going back to the expectations you wrote down and seeing if those training expectations were met in the time allotted. Continue to improve the training as needed. Every time innovation occurs in the company, all training programs should be updated as needed, immediately. When ever possible, training department as well as each manager's OJT programs, should be accessible electronically to facilitate keeping the learning current. Innovative companies enjoy easy-to-use, updated systems.

Many of us inherit the staff we have and often there are no communicated measurable performance expectations. Due to lack of documentation, we may be unsure if or how our inherited staff was trained. Whenever performance is consistently below standard, it is important to determine if the person needs training. If the individual is not able to demonstrate the basic skills or procedures needed to do the job, training should be provided. If the individual has been formally trained, begin coaching to help bring performance to standard. If performance does not improve after providing training and coaching, she/he is likely not suited to the job.

What do you think of the following scenario: Henry has just come on board. Sam, his new boss, is preparing Henry for training. Let's listen in:

Sam: I'm going to spend a few minutes explaining what your training will consist of and then answer any questions or discuss any issues or concerns you might have. Is that OK with you?

Henry: Sure, Sam.

Sam: The objective or result expected from our department is to keep customers coming back to continue or do more business with us and refer others to us. We measure those results in random customer surveys by mail, phone, and at the counter. This year, our department, and each individual in it, must achieve a minimum rating of 7 on a scale of 1 to 10, where 10 is the highest. Here is an example of the customer satisfaction survey so you can see what we measure and how scores are derived. Our performance expectations are high, as you learned during your interview, and we expect everyone on the team to achieve a consistent 7.0 or better on the surveys. Last year our team averaged 6.8 when the standard was 6.5 and so far this year the team average is 7.1. Everyone is very proud and works at getting better.

To see how our team achieves those results, your first two days of training will be observing Andy today and Jill on Tuesday. They are two of our trainers and were advanced to trainer positions because they each consistently achieve 8.5+ on the customer and team surveys. Please watch and listen to two things during these observation days with your trainers: first their interaction with the customers and co-workers and next what actions they take. I'll meet with you and your trainer each day at 12:00 for lunch. Then I'll meet with you again, alone, at 5:15 in the afternoon, knowing you leave at 5:30 p.m. Each time we meet, be prepared to tell me what you observed about the trainers' interactions with customers and co-workers and actions taken. Ask as many questions as you wish. How does that sound?

Henry: Sounds fine, but where do I find Andy and Jill?

Sam: Great question. Actually, I'll be taking you out to the department after your company orientation is completed around 10:00 this morning. You'll be introduced to the team and given your desk, where you can relax a few minutes and get yourself organized before Andy comes to get you at 10:30. Jill will meet you at your desk on Tuesday morning when you arrive at 8:30. Do you have any questions?

Henry: No, not right now. Just be ready to discuss interactions with customers and co-workers and actions taken, right?

Sam: Exactly. OK, let's get you to orientation on time. Our HR manager, Manuel Costa, is a terrific person to know and is very helpful when we need to know about benefits, safety, and all kinds of important information. He'll be introducing you to many of these things this morning. You'll be in orientation about an hour. Hi, Manny, this is Henry, and he is ready for orientation. Henry, I'll see you at 10:00.

What did you like about Sam's approach? _____

_____

_____

_____

What would you do differently? _____

_____

_____

_____

Let's explore training more deeply by visiting with Martha in the case study that follows.

Case Study 1

Martha knows after hiring and training more than a dozen employees in the last three years, that it takes no more than thirty days on average for someone to do the job. Every new employee spends one full week in training and within thirty days knows the job. Martha's training is very structured and consists of day 1, company orientation, and then she assigns the trainee to a "training buddy." All eight people on Martha's team do the same job so they are all expected to participate in training duty and Martha keeps a rotation schedule of all their participation. Everyone in the department knows that the week she/he has training duty, goals are waived for the designated trainer so everyone else has to pick up the slack to be sure department goals are met for the week. In those weeks, department goals are usually not met.

During the afternoons of day 1 and 2, the trainee observes the training buddy. On days 3 and 4, the trainee performs the work while the trainer teammate watches and tells the trainee what to do when she/he makes a mistake. On day 5, the trainee works alone and asks the training buddy for help only when needed. This method has been working fine as far as Martha is concerned. Martha's manager has expressed concern on many occasions that customer complaints have been growing about the services her department performs and has been telling Martha she needs to do something about it. Martha always informs her manager that the customers are simply not patient enough with the new people and she keeps telling the chronic complainers to just call her if they have a problem and she will take care of it.

Martha's development plan for over a year now has had the goal of reducing turnover. She has been supervising a team of eight people for the last three years and cannot imagine what the problem is. It's just the nature of the job that makes employees want to leave within a year. On average, employees leave after eight months. She can't seem to help her manager understand that this is just the way it is and she has it under control. After all, Martha is very good at attracting new employees and usually fills vacant positions within four to five weeks of a person leaving.

1. What elements of Martha's training program help new employees learn?

_____

_____

_____

2. How does the training possibly contribute to customer service problems?

_____

_____

_____

3. How does the training possibly contribute to turnover?

_____

_____

_____

4. What would you do differently to train new hires?

_____

_____

_____

SAMPLE TRAINING PLAN

Select a job you supervise and prepare a training plan for one of the major responsibilities of that job.

Position:_____   **Task:**_____

Training Date:_____

What are the steps of the task to be accomplished (list in order):

Step 1:_____

Step 2: _____

Step 3: _____

Step 4: _____

Step 5: _____

Step 6:_____

Step 7: _____

Step 8: _____

Step 9: _____

Step 10: _____

What results will I tell trainees to look for so they will recognize results expected when the skills/task is done correctly?

_____

_____

_____

How will I make sure trainees can identify critical steps of the task performed correctly and in proper sequence?

_____

_____

_____

What will I ask trainees to do that will show they can demonstrate critical skills/task performed correctly and in proper sequence?

_____

_____

_____

Measured Results: Trainee was able to:

1. Recognize results expected when the skills/task is done correctly:

Yes ___ No___

2. Identify critical steps of the task performed correctly and in proper sequence:

Yes___ No___

3. Demonstrate critical skills/task performed correctly and in proper sequence:

Yes___ No___

Date_____   Trainee Initials _____   Manager Initials_____

How PREPARED Are You to TRAIN?

On a scale of 1 to 10 (10 = highest) rate yourself on how well you do each of the following:

Rating

_____ I ensure each member of my team knows the performance expected of her/him and the team in total.

_____ I let the new hires know what the expectations are, *what* is expected of them by *when*, and work closely with them to train, coach, and monitor their progress.

_____ I tell or show my trainees what to expect as a result of the skill/task being done correctly. They know the expected outcome to look for.

_____ I demonstrate a task in order and correctly until my trainees can consistently identify the critical steps performed in proper sequence.

_____ Trainees keep a list of the top five most common errors and how to avoid them. They actually write these down when they recognize the error during training and use it as a reference tool later.

_____ After observing a demonstration, I ask the trainee to write down or flowchart the steps to complete the task, then compare their response to what I have prepared. The trainee can then determine if she/he included all steps in order, etc. Demonstration continues until the trainee identifies all steps.

_____ My trainees must be able to consistently demonstrate the *critical* skills/task performed correctly and in proper sequence before I let them do the job on their own.

_____ When I anticipate or see a trainee make an error, unless it would cause something terrible to happen that cannot be corrected easily, I do not interrupt or point it out. Yes, I let them make mistakes.

_____ When trainees make an error, I ask them to identify the error, what caused it and how to correct it. It is a great way to teach them to be problem solvers.

_____ My employee turnover rate is below company average.

_____ **TOTAL** ÷ 10 = _____.   Circle your score:

1--1.5--2--2.5--3--3.5--4--4.5--5--5.5--6--6.5--7--7.5--8--8.5--9--9.5--10

Not Prepared   Somewhat Prepared   Well Prepared

Coaching

Coaching provides guidance and direction to ensure information and skills required to do the job are implemented properly in order to meet performance expectations.

Successful managers ensure team members are trained properly in the information and skills needed to do the job in order to meet expectations. Next, they spend most of their time coaching and developing each team member on implementation of what they learned to meet and exceed those expectations. Now that you have a good idea of how properly conducted training can solve the first piece of the performance improvement puzzle, let's focus on coaching to solve the second piece.

Building on information and skills learned in training and guiding overall performance to help someone reach or exceed performance expectations is what makes coaching one of the greatest and most powerful responsibilities of a manager. When referring to coaching as powerful, here is where the "power" comes in. If the average employee is continuously coached to use the skills needed to do the job in an effective manner, the opportunity for that employee to achieve and even exceed standard performance can be as high as 80%. Now that is POWER! Is 80% of your staff meeting or exceeding expectations?

The inverse is also true. There is a less than 20% chance on average that a newly learned skill will be implemented and developed into a correctly performed habit when little or no coaching is provided.

On average, successful managers plan for forty hours of basic and advanced training for their employees annually and plan 50% of their own time dedicated to coaching their employees to improve performance. These top-performing managers are very skilled at coaching and they love doing it. They want to spend their time coaching because that is what produces the greatest rewards for them, the employee, the team, and the company.

Just think! Out of the average work year consisting of approximately 2,000 hours, a good manager spends 1,000 hours or more dedicated to coaching team members to perform their tasks at or above standard.

It usually takes thirty to ninety days of continuous use for a new skill to become habit. Every time we train an employee in a new skill or task, it takes thirty to ninety days, depending upon complexity and prior experience, for the new skill or task to be implemented by that employee in a way that becomes comfortable and habitual. Coaching is the guidance and direction the manager provides to ensure the skills are implemented properly and good habits are forming. Left to their own devices, your very resourceful employees will find innovative, comfortable ways to use what they learned, right or wrong.

Training normally covers lots of information, new skills, and processes. Unless we are practicing and being coached in each step until we can use it effortlessly, we often do not remember everything we are taught. That is normal and is often called the "use or lose" theory. If a manager does not begin to coach to each step or skill immediately after training is complete, chances are the employee will lose most of what she/he was trained in. There goes the possible 80% return. *What a waste!*

Some managers do little or no coaching. When asked why, they often say, "I let my employees be creative. They are more likely to find new and better ways of performing the job if they don't have me on their back. They develop their own style."

This is a familiar trap that any manager can easily fall into. Good coaching is about helping employees meet or exceed performance expectations. Good coaching is about knowing what fundamentals work to achieve expectations and letting employees who are creative, improve upon what works. This is where creativity shines because individuals who can take what works and improve upon it, are raising performance expectations in a way that can be used to train and coach others to do the same. Creativity for its own sake has little value. Creativity for the sake of raising productivity has great value.

Style is simply an individual's way of behaving in a comfortable manner. Most of us adopt a style until we develop our own. If you were going to play tennis, you would first learn the fundamental strokes and the rules of the game. As you grew more comfortable with performing the steps correctly, you might naturally add your own style to the fundamentals. This is creative and will work, as long as your style does not impede your ability to win some games.

Often, when a manager is coaching a resistant, below-standard employee in the fundamentals needed to reach standard, the employee will say, "That's not my style." Encourage the employee to reach standard first by applying the fundamentals and then use her/his style to exceed it.

Employees unaccustomed to being coached are often not comfortable having a manager work with them. Managers must be sensitive to each person's behavioral traits and learning type. Personal profile tools, which are often used as part of the hiring process, can also be used to identify communication styles to enhance dialogue. Two very good personal profile tools are the **PPS** or *Personal Profile System*, designed to be self-administered and self-scored (www.trainingsolutions.com), and the **PPA** *Personal Profile Analysis,* which can be administered electronically and provides an invaluable debriefing by a trained professional (www.thomasinternational.net). To learn more about what these tools can do, I encourage you to visit these sites.

A well-thought-out and openly discussed *Performance Improvement Action Plan*, based upon the need to reach specific standards, is a great way to help break the ice and begin to coach and work effectively together.

ABCD's of Coaching

Coaching does not have to be complicated. Actually, to be most effective, it should be very simple. One method for coaching that is simple to follow is the **ABCD** method:

A = ACTION

Take continuous action by creating and following up on *Performance Improvement Action Plans*, at least weekly for new or below-standard performers, at least quarterly for at or above standard performers.

B = BE INVOLVED

Be involved in those development plans by including what coaching actions you will take. Examples of being involved include:

– Consistently demonstrating the behavior you wish the employee to emulate.

– Role-playing to help practice, develop, upgrade performance.

– Observing the employee on the job.

C = CHECK

Check *Performance Improvement Action Plans* are being worked and results are being achieved. Follow up.

D = DOCUMENT

Document the employee's *Performance Improvement Action Plan* progress and keep copies of completed plans in the employee's personnel file for reference.

Being an effective manager would probably not be considered easy, but for most of us, it is challenging and rewarding. What can make the job less difficult and more rewarding is coaching on a consistent basis. Coaching with the help of the **ABCD** method is one way to do just that. After all, it is the ability of each member of your team to perform at or above standard that will allow you to reach or exceed your department or team goals. The manager can either spend precious time trying to do it all or spend that same time helping the team learn to do it correctly, and together. It is much easier to reach your goals when everyone on the team is consistently contributing to the results. The good coach helps make that happen.

As seen in professional sports, good coaches are rarely the superstars who got promoted. Superstars often struggle as coaches because they like the limelight (doing things their own way), and most often believe no one else can do anything as well as they do it. Because someone is great at performing most of the tasks within a department does not mean that person would make it as a manager.

To be a good people manager requires someone who consistently and successfully implements the three management success factors:

1. Recruiting and hiring the best people for the job.

2. Training and coaching all to meet the performance expectations of the job.

3. Conducting performance reviews often, fairly, positively, and on time.

Most great coaches know what tasks and skills are required to do each job they oversee and understand the relationship between performing those tasks and meeting the performance expectations.

Great coaches most often did the job or jobs they now directly supervise and performed them to standard or just above standard very consistently. They were usually eager to learn new things and were always coming up with ideas to improve the processes within the department to make the job easier, quicker, better. It is likely they achieved results for the customer, exercised good judgment when dealing with teammates, and always acted professionally.

Have you ever watched a professional basketball or football game and witnessed a coach running onto the playing surface and jumping into the game? Probably not. These coaches ensure each player is trained in the basic skills and rules of the game at training camp. Then they direct and guide performance improvement all year long during practice, coaching sessions, and breaks in the game. When the game is in play, they let the individuals perform to the best of their ability. As the play goes on, coaches constantly observe each individual's performance and the team as a whole. They never seem to miss a practice or game and prefer this observation activity to being in their office. Most of a coach's time is spent watching, listening, and determining:

1. when appreciation should be shown (*compliment a team member publicly for a specific task done right*)

2. where a performance correction needs to be made (*take a team member aside and remind her/him of the right method to be used*)

3. what team interaction needs to be smoothed out (*meet with the team to discuss how more effective interaction will improve the game and help the team to win*)

4. when and what level of discipline is needed (*take a team member aside and let her/him know when a specific behavior or attitude will not be tolerated because it violates policy or procedure, is impacting the team or a team member's ability to work, or is consistently not up to standard*)

A coach's behavior in the workplace should be very much the same as it is in professional sports.

Let's go to **Case Study 2** and look in on our manager, Martha, to see how she is doing.

Case Study 2

Six months ago, Martha found herself with a new manager. This manager spent a lot of time working with Martha on improving her managerial skills in order for Martha to meet new performance expectations. These expectations included turnover under 20% and customer satisfaction ratings of 8 or better, where the highest is 10. Her new manager made it very clear these expectations must be met or exceeded consistently for Martha's performance to be considered satisfactory. But the manager also made it clear that Martha would receive training and coaching to help her be successful. This was hard to hear, yet the new manager stayed very positive and worked hard with Martha to help her succeed. She even encouraged Martha to take advantage of two training programs: one on how to recruit and hire employees that match the needs of the job; and one on how to train and coach employees more effectively, where she learned the importance of communicating performance expectations to the team and measuring results.

As Martha worked through the training, she and her manager created and worked on *Performance Improvement Action Plan*s for each step in the process. The manager trained Martha until she was able to perform each of these tasks properly. Then she coached her until she was comfortable performing the tasks correctly without having to think about them. Martha liked the process and found herself implementing the same training and coaching methods with her team that her manager was using with her.

Over the next six months, Martha experienced only one of the eight on her team leaving, or 12.5% turnover, and had a department customer satisfaction rating of 8.9. Martha felt great about meeting and beating her expectations. She felt bad about losing the person but good about doing everything she could to help the person reach the performance expectations. She kept excellent documentation on what did or did not work and why. She knew by now how to train and coach to help each employee. But she also knew she could not *make* any employee perform to standard. Getting the job done would always be the responsibility of each employee. Being a good manager who can hire, train, and coach effectively was her responsibility and she wasn't going to succeed unless her employees did.

What did Martha's new manager do differently (from her previous manager) to help her? _____

_____

How did this benefit Martha? _____

_____

How did this benefit Martha's staff? _____

_____

What do you believe were the greatest contributors to Martha's success?

_____

_____

Why do you think Martha has a new manager? _____

_____

Discipline

Occasionally, members of your team may require discipline. Providing it is part of being the coach and goes with the job. Most managers do not like to discipline their staff and many actually avoid it. When asked, many will tell you they do not like disciplining employees because they do not like being confrontational.

One thing we all know for sure is that sticking your head in the sand, hoping poor behavior will go away, doesn't work. Not only does it not work, it usually means you will have a long-term, reoccurring problem on your hands. It also sends the message to the entire team that there are no negative consequences for poor performance or inappropriate behavior.

Discipline is not the same as terminating an employee. Discipline is an action that focuses on correcting a specific performance problem. If done properly and soon after the behavior occurs, you may be pleased to discover that the employee quickly shows improvement.

Learning to discipline in an appropriate and consistent manner (based on what level of discipline other employees received for the same offense) actually works to *reduce* the level of confrontation and ultimately makes supervising much easier. You can probably think of an example in your own experience that proved it to you.

Discipline may be required when:

- Attitude, attendance, and/or behavior violate company policies and procedures.

- Attitude, attendance, and/or behavior are negatively impacting the team or another team member's ability to work.

- Performance is consistently below standard and training and coaching have not helped.

Coaching on how and when to apply discipline is extremely valuable. Your manager, HR department or coaching professional should be consulted. Discipline is rarely easy and fraught with employee relations mines. You should not take it lightly. Seek coaching help whenever you need it.

Using correct and consistent procedures when disciplining any employee can help you maintain an atmosphere employees want to work in, supports good morale, and can help you reduce excessive turnover.

Some level of discipline would be required for attitude, attendance and/or behavior that:

- Violates company policy or procedure

- Is consistently not up to standard

- Negatively impacts the team or a team member's ability to work

Remember, once the decision has been made to discipline an employee, the most important factor to consider is what level of discipline other employees have received for the same offense.

Again, discipline is not the same as terminating an employee. Discipline is an action that focuses on correcting a specific performance. Think about an example from your own experience or observation of when appropriate and consistent discipline worked. Write it down. Every time you consider avoiding this important coaching responsibility, you can come back here, look at your example, and remember why you need to provide appropriate and consistent discipline.

What have you learned so far?

What are the two pieces to the puzzle of how to improve your team's performance?

_____

_____

What is the difference between training and coaching?

Training _____ .

Coaching _____ .

What two outcomes usually occur when someone is not coached after training?

_____

OR

_____

Successful training and coaching rely heavily on knowing what the
_____ _____ are and applying all skills, learning, practice, implementation, and development to achieving them.

If a manager does not coach to what is trained, the employee will most likely lose the recently learned information or skill. This is what we call the "_____ or _____" theory.

Define what each element of the ABCD method of coaching stands for:

A_____

B_____

C_____

D_____

Most of the coach's time is spent watching, listening, and determining:

When to show _____

Where a _____

What team _____

When and what level of _____

Discipline is the same as terminating. True or False? _____

Discipline may be required when any one of these three things occurs:

Attitude, attendance, and/or behavior_____.

Attitude, attendance and/or behavior are negatively _____.

Performance is consistently_____.

Whose responsibility is it to train and coach? _____.

Check your answers on the next page.

What have you learned so far? (Answers)

What are the two pieces to the puzzle of how to improve your team's performance?

Training and Coaching.

What is the difference between training and coaching?

Training provides guided learning of information and practice of skills needed to do a job.

Coaching provides *on-the-job* guidance and direction to ensure information and skills learned in training are implemented properly in order to meet performance expectations.

What two outcomes usually occur when someone is not coached after training?

Employees find a way to do the job that feels comfortable even if it isn't what was taught. OR employees quit and go work somewhere else.

Successful training and coaching rely heavily on knowing what the *performance expectations* are and applying all skills, learning, practice, implementation and development to achieving them.

If a manager does not coach to what is trained, the employee will most likely lose the recently learned information or skill. This is called the "use or lose" theory.

Define what each element of the ABCD method of coaching stand for:

Action
Be involved
Check
Document

Most of the coach's time is spent watching, listening, and determining:

When to show appreciation.

Where a performance correction needs to be made.

What team interaction needs to be smoothed out.

When and what level of discipline is needed.

Discipline is the same as terminating. True or False? <u>False</u>

Discipline may be required when:

Attitude, attendance, and/or behavior violate policy or procedure of the company.

Attitude, attendance and/or behavior are negatively impacting the team or a team member's ability to work.

Performance is consistently below standard and training and coaching have not helped.

Whose responsibility is it to train and coach? <u>The manager.</u>

How PREPARED Are You to COACH?

On a scale of 1 to 10 (10 = highest) rate yourself on how well you do each of the following:

Rating

_____ I ensure my team knows the performance expected.

_____ After my employees complete any training program, I immediately hand them a *Performance Improvement Action Plan* and spend a few moments working with them on ways we will work together to ensure they develop good habits using what they just learned.

_____ I coach my staff on the fundamentals needed to meet performance expectations, so they will stay on track to consistently reach and perform at or above standard.

_____ I jot down a note when I see behavior *consistently above standard* and keep it on file so I won't forget.

_____ When coaching, I employ an ABCD approach: **A**ction, **B**e involved, **C**heck, **D**ocument.

_____ I compliment a team member publicly when a task is done right.

_____ When I see an incorrect behavior, I take a team member aside and remind her/him of the correct behavior.

_____ Any time team interaction needs to be smoothed out, I meet with the team to discuss how more effective interaction will improve the team's ability to meet expectations and achieve goals.

_____ Whenever a team member's behavior violates policy or procedure, impacts another team member or the team's ability to work, or performance is consistently below standard and training and coaching have not helped, I administer discipline in a consistent and fair manner in an attempt to correct the behavior.

_____ My employee turnover rate is below company average.

_____ **TOTAL** ÷ 10 = _____.   Circle your score:

1--1.5--2--2.5--3--3.5--4--4.5--5--5.5--6--6.5--7--7.5--8--8.5--9--9.5--10

Not Prepared   Somewhat Prepared   Well Prepared

Measuring and Communicating

Managers should always be in the process of developing their staff. Good coaching means the manager and employee continuously work together on specific *Performance Improvement Action Plans* to improve performance in particular areas. Coaching provides the important opportunity to keep each team member aware of her/his performance and helps ensure expectations are being met on a continuing basis.

Effective managers do not wait for the formal performance review to sit down and talk candidly with an individual about performance and write up *Performance Improvement Action Plans* accordingly. After all, the performance review is an event. Coaching is a process. These good managers are doing this critical part of their job continuously and placing copies of the *Performance Improvement Action Plans* and results achieved in each individual's personnel file for reference when the next formal review is due.

Good coaching managers communicate their expectations and keep good measurement records of how each employee is meeting, exceeding or falling below those expectations. These managers know how hard it is to accurately remember all the important information about each employee's performance. They set aside a few minutes at least weekly for new employees and at least quarterly for consistently standard and above-standard performers. Together they reflect on and document progress on the current *Performance Improvement Action Plan.*

Managers must strive to stay focused on performance associated with meeting each expectation. This is one way to help stay objective and consistent.

Measuring is the objective tracking of progress toward an expected outcome.

Communicating is the means of sharing information, expectations, status, and results.

Scenario 1: JD has been working in this specific position for three months now. Over that time, the manager has complimented JD at least two or three times on the work accomplished. This week the manager called a team meeting and told everyone that the vice president is upset because productivity is not good enough. The manager says everyone must work harder and accomplish more or the department's annual goals will not be reached, and heads will roll. JD thinks: "I'm working as hard as possible already. I don't know how to accomplish more without incurring overtime, which the department does not allow. Why do I have to hear this? I don't get it. My manager has only complimented my work and never told me I was not working hard enough. Well, I can't work any harder. But, I must be OK. After all, I know of at least two other employees in my department that goof off all the time. This little talk must have been for their benefit, not mine." A week later, the manager calls JD into the office and delivers this reprimand: "You are not working as hard as everyone else on the team and you have got to get your act together. Do we understand each other?" JD simply says yes, and walks out of the office fuming, embarrassed, and very confused.

Why does this happen? If you understand what measuring productivity and communicating status and results can do to improve performance, it does not have to happen. Let's change the scenario a little and look for the difference.

Scenario 2: JD has been working in this specific position for three months now. In the first few weeks, JD was trained in the job and told what the performance expectations were. It was reinforced that within the first ninety days standard performance should be consistently achieved. The manager complimented JD two or three times on very specific work accomplished, and was coaching JD on two areas of responsibility where performance was not consistently up to standard yet. With coaching, JD's work was reaching standard more often but not consistently. This week the manager met with each team member *individually*. In the meetings with standard and above-standard performers, each was asked for suggestions on ways strong team members might help others stay on target. One suggestion was to ask the manager to post weekly individual performances to standard rather than just the overall team performance. That way they could all see where everyone on the team was strong and where some might be struggling. They could then try to help struggling teammates find ways to improve. The meetings with each below-standard but improving performers like JD went a little differently. They were told once again how important it was that expectations be met every week, discussed coaching plan progress, and spoke very openly about consequences of not consistently meeting standard. Then the manager discussed the suggestions given by the strong performers and asked which might help that person the most. Everyone was told the suggestion the *majority preferred* would be implemented. The next day the manager called a quick team meeting, told the group the suggestion for *posting individual performance to goal* was approved by the majority, and agreed to try it for one week. A team meeting was set for next week, same day and time, to discuss how it was working. JD met the expectations all that week. Consistent performance to standard was reinforced in the manager's next coaching sessions with JD and plans were made to reach above standard performance. JD's performance has been at or above standard consistently ever since.

Analyzing the problem:

1. What were the main differences you noticed between scenario 1 and 2?

_____

_____

_____

2. What do you feel contributed to JD's accomplishing a first week of consistent standard performance?

_____

_____

_____

3. What do you feel contributed to JD's accomplishing consistent long-term at and above-standard performance?

_____

_____

_____

4. What would you have done differently if you were the manager in this situation?

_____

_____

_____

Measuring is the objective tracking of progress toward an expected outcome.

In the world of work there are always expectations to be met. Measuring progress along the way tells us if we are hitting benchmarks that show we are on track to reach the expected results or goal.

What would life be like if no one measured anything? What would happen to education, sports, medical treatment, and business, just for starters? Think of what might happen if you set a goal, i.e., "I want to accomplish these eight projects in the next six months." However, you did not set benchmarks or measure your progress along the way to ensure you were completing those projects at a pace that would allow you to get to your goal on time. Measuring is necessary to determine where we are in relationship to our expectations and our goals. Without it, we can easily get lost.

One of the main reasons businesses and managers struggle and sometimes fail is because progress is not monitored early and frequently enough. Often the owner or manager is very busy doing the things she/he likes most. These 'things" are often the reasons they went into the business or a job in the first place, like wanting to own a store or having the opportunity to supervise a department. By owning or supervising we can grow and, even better, have an opportunity to "do it our way." For some it may be the chance to show the world they know better how to treat customers or hire more qualified employees or select more desirable merchandise, and on and on.

Unfortunately the reality of the day-to-day job is often so consuming, it is easy to lose sight of what it takes to keep the business on track to meet its overall business goals. When this is the case, it's even easier to avoid the things that many of us consider the not so fun parts of the job, like establishing performance expectations, setting measurement criteria and then actively and constantly measuring progress toward meeting those expectations.

When daily pressures get in our way, we end up not measuring progress to goal often enough. What we frequently learn too late is that the ability to achieve our goals in the time allotted has now disappeared. Our goal is suddenly out of our reach. When our boss comes calling at the end of the month and asks why the expected goals were not reached in time, the echoing answer is the one they dislike most, yet hear most often. "Things just got away from me."

If it's your first experience not meeting an expectation, your manager usually gives you another chance. And, if you're lucky, your manager will coach you in setting up the measurement criteria and the monitoring frequency and ask you to report measurement daily or weekly so "things don't just get away from you," again. If you are unlucky, and unfortunately this is more the norm, your manager tells you in a voice you have never heard this person use before, "Next month you better achieve the sum total of what you didn't reach this month, plus all of next month's goals – or else!" Then she/ he storms out the door never to be heard from again until the end of next month.

Let's not dwell on the negatives. Let's discuss more positive thoughts. Achieving, winning, being successful, and meeting and exceeding expectations are all more positive places to be than the alternatives. The story is more positive to tell, too. It's even much easier to feel positive and have some fun if you know you are reaching goals.

Successful people, who take management positions to have direct impact on growing or improving the business, actually might be having fun. The secret is staying focused on the goals and keeping a close eye on your team's progress toward reaching those goals. Now if that sounds to you like it is easier or at least a lot more positive than the uncomfortable alternative, you would be right. In the long run, doing things right the first time and staying on that positive track usually proves to be much easier and more comfortable for you and everyone on your team, including your boss.

The first and most critical step is to know what your department expectations are and to be sure you and your manager are in agreement on what they are. Each individual's job expectations should directly relate to department expectations, which in turn directly link to company goals. Imagine the consequences of everyone having her/his own agenda and going off in different directions with different and likely conflicting goals.

We are talking about feeling positive here. Using all that good energy to get to the wrong place doesn't sound or feel very positive. So making sure you, your manager and your team are heading toward the same goal is critical.

Setting Expectations and Measuring Progress

Before we can set performance expectations and help our team meet them, it is helpful to test our own ability to set expectations for ourselves. Managers who find it difficult to set clear, measurable expectations or are uncomfortable with using expectations as a way to manage the productivity and goal-reaching ability of their team are likely to have the same difficulty or discomfort when doing the same for themselves.

Delegating work to others can be difficult sometimes. If you are concerned that delegating important work responsibilities to your team means the work will not get done right or on time, then you need to think hard about your role as a manager. It may have a lot to do with how you are progressing with your true responsibilities of training and coaching. It is the manager's responsibility to see that the team meets its expectations. This can be done by ensuring everyone is trained to do the job correctly and coaching each person continuously to meet and exceed the performance expectations to guarantee goals are met. Teach and coach others to do all the "important work" and then, when they are doing a good job or maybe even a better job than you did, congratulate them for good work and congratulate yourself for doing the job of a manager.

Now let's move on to a little management ingredient that can surely make the cake of success rise or fall. This is measuring progress at intervals to ensure actual performance will reach goal in the time allotted. Take interim measurements of your progress to goal using *Performance Improvement Action Plans*.

If most of your team is meeting the expectations, then it may be time to challenge their ability to improve upon the way things are being done. A solid performing group is very capable of creatively finding ways to increase productivity and outpace the old expectations. This helps your team constantly improve productivity without your having to demand it. If expectations are going up, this means everyone's performance is going up and should be a great source of pride for the team.

Raising expectations becomes a penalty when the majority of team member's performance is below standard and yet goals are increasing and more productivity is required from those same people. Caution signs should flash and red flags should wave if this occurs. It is critical for the manager to determine if productivity has maxed out and more people are needed to handle increased work volume or if performance has leveled or dropped off. The answer is, most often, the latter.

Most people want to and will do a good job more often if they know what is expected and are trained and coached to meet and then exceed the expectations. This helps create a motivational environment where exceeding expectations, hence high productivity, becomes the norm for the group. If you coach, you can more often remain on the sidelines, communicating and measuring performance, while letting them succeed.

Measuring Case Study: Harry's boss informs him as he leaves work Friday that customers are complaining about lag time, so his department must now complete all requests received in forty-eight hours or less. Harry's group has been completing all requests within three to five days most of the time and a little longer only during busy times. Over the weekend Harry considers what to do to comply with this new directive. The team is going to be upset, but he is only the messenger, right? Harry figures he'll just tell everyone the new deadlines, tell them they must work faster, and then everything will be OK.

A few weeks later the boss asks Harry why complaints are still coming in about request lag time. Harry is at a loss. He tells the boss that he told everyone what was expected and things seemed to be working. Now there were a few days that there were so many requests it was impossible to complete them all in the forty-eight hours. But they got done in seventy-two hours, which was fantastic time. And, after all, they can't stop everybody from complaining. With some people, it's just their nature. The boss agrees and says, "We'll talk more about this later," and rushes off to a meeting.

At the next monthly meeting, Harry's boss talks about each area in the call-in department and puts up a chart showing stats about each one of them. When she gets to Harry's request area – before she puts up the chart – she asks Harry how many requests his group gets a week. Harry says he is not exactly positive but estimates around 400-500. Harry's boss puts up his chart and it looks something like this:

Week # 14

589	requests
120	processed 24 hrs
350	processed 48 hours
119	processed +48 hrs
20%	over expected time
52	# complaints
9%	% complaints to requests

Week # 15

606	requests
117	processed 24 hrs
312	processed 48 hours
177	processed +48 hrs
29%	over expected time
73	# complaints
12%	% complaints to requests

Week # 16

522	requests
104	processed 24 hrs
275	processed 48 hours
143	processed +48 hrs
27%	over expected time
61	# complaints
11%	% complaints to requests

Week # 17

566	requests
110	processed 24 hrs
250	processed 48 hours
206	processed +48 hrs
36%	over expected time
68	# complaints
12%	% complaints to requests

Harry's boss is angry with the number of complaints and says so. Harry is uncomfortable when he sees the numbers and is very angry his boss didn't show him this information weeks ago. Now he looks like an idiot in front of the other managers, whose charted numbers seemed to be fine.

What were the performance expectations that needed to be met?

_____

_____

What observations can you draw from the chart?

_____

_____

Specific to measuring performance, what would you do differently than Harry? _____

_____

Specific to measuring performance, what would you do differently than Harry's boss?

_____

_____

Communicating: The Key to Retention

Communicating is the means of sharing information, expectations, status, and results.

Most members of your team need your help to stay motivated day after day. A great contributor to maintaining a motivated team is frequent, consistent, and meaningful communication. Being kept informed of where the team and individuals are in relationship to the team's objectives helps keep everyone involved and participating.

One of the major reasons people cite in exit interviews for leaving employment is "lack of communication from my manager." HR staff members often see or hear in exit interviews comments like, "My manager hardly talked to me and didn't listen when I tried to talk," or "I never knew where I stood," or "I never felt I was making any contribution to the success of the team." When HR shares these comments with managers, it is important to take this helpful information seriously. Retaining good employees has everything to do with the manager's ability to foster positive, meaningful communication. It is important for all of us to know what is expected, how we are doing relative to expectations, and what our role is in helping our department and the company continuously reach growth and improvement goals.

Communication also means listening to our employees. It's easy to listen when you like what someone is saying. How good are you at listening when you have little interest or do not like the person? All of us are very busy and often find ourselves listening on the run. How do employees feel when we avoid conversation or relegate its importance to "you have less than thirty seconds before my next conference call"? How would you feel?

Communication consistency is another very important consideration. Do you communicate with each member of your team in a similar fashion? Do you greet everyone when you come in mornings, or just your buddy? Do you give everyone the information they need to know on where they stand or only those who are doing a great job?

Communication is a wonderful tool and should be used to its fullest. Tools get rusty when we don't use them often. Take a moment now to think about how you communicate. What do you like about your communication with your team? What could you improve on?

Keep communication simple. Visibly post team goals and performance expectations; privately discuss (and document) individual goals and expectations. Visibly post team results; privately discuss (and document) individual results.

How much time would it take to do these two things? Not much. If you did only these two things, and did them at least quarterly and consistently with every team member, you would be amazed at the difference in your team's morale and productivity. Think about it. Most of what is needed to accomplish posting the information is probably available on reports you already use or receive or have access to. That's one way to save time. Use what is already available.

Now it is just a matter of setting aside the time to actually do it. Posting team goals, expectations, progress, and results needs to be done only once a day or weekly or monthly, depending on your business, expectations, and measurement criteria. Monthly would be a great start.

The "talking to the individual" part of the communication is where we seem to spend the least time and yet it is the most critical. One of the quickest and easiest ways to fulfill this important responsibility is to use *Performance Improvement Action Plans* with every team member. Consider this. Let's say you have five people reporting to you. Two of them are consistently meeting or exceeding standard. You could meet with the two standard and above-standard performers at least quarterly and prepare together an action plan to help each of them improve on current performance. That is only sixty minutes maximum per quarter, given thirty minutes per person. Now schedule the times on your calendar and tell these two employees to do the same.

The three below-standard employees should meet with you at least weekly, because if their performance does not meet standard within a reasonable and consistent time frame, they will no longer be on the team. So it is critical to them and to you to work closely on action plans and do everything you can to help as they strive to consistently meet the expectations. The sooner this happens, the sooner you can meet with them quarterly, and save all that time for other coaching opportunities. So let's see how much time this will take:

Three below-standard employees X 30 minutes each = 90 minutes or 1.5 hours each week.

Of the forty+ hours spent working in five days, this represents only 4% of your time. Your time management skills now come into play to ensure you set aside ninety minutes or 4% of each week (ninety minutes on one day or thirty minutes a day for three days of the week) to keep good communication.

Here is how good time management works. Write the meetings on your calendar, notify your employees of when their meetings are scheduled, and then keep the meetings. If you have trouble with time management, see your manager for coaching assistance or attend a one-day course. A quick solution is to stop at the library or bookstore at lunch and check out a book on the subject. There are lots of good ones available. After all, your ability to reach and exceed your department goals depends upon how well your people do their job. Coaching everyone on your team to perform to and above standard is your job. This is the minimum time it takes. You can do this.

To start, you can keep communication simple by doing the following two things once per month:

1. Visibly post team goals and performance expectations; privately discuss (and document) individual goals and expectations.

2. Visibly post team results; privately discuss (and document) individual results.

Doing just these two things consistently can make an immense difference in your team's productivity and morale.

On an ongoing basis, how much time do you need to communicate effectively?

\# standard and above-standard employees X 30 min. **quarterly** =____min.

\# below-standard employees X 30 min. **weekly** = ____ min.

Can you do this?

If yes, will you do this?

On a scale from 1 (excellent) to 5 (need help), rate yourself as a listener.

_____Do I allow the speaker to express her/his complete thoughts without interrupting?

_____Do I listen between the lines, especially when conversing with individuals who frequently use hidden meanings?

_____Do I actively try to develop retention ability to remember important facts?

_____Do I write down the most important details of a message?

_____In recording a message, do I concentrate on writing the major facts and key phrases?

_____Do I say or read essential details back to the speaker before the conversation ends to ensure correct understanding?

_____Do I refrain from turning off the speaker because the message is dull or boring or because I do not personally know or like the speaker?

_____Do I avoid becoming hostile or excited when a speaker's views differ from my own?

_____Do I ignore distractions when listening (phone ringing, people interrupting)?

_____Do I express a genuine interest in the other individual's conversation?

_____**TOTAL** ÷ 10 = _____.   Circle your score:

1-2 = good skill development

3 = few needs areas to work on

4.5 = set an action plan to improve

What have you learned so far?

Four ingredients of how to improve your team's performance:

a. _____

b. _____

c. _____

d. _____

What is the difference between measuring and communicating?

Measuring is _____

Communicating is _____

Most members of your team need your help to stay motivated day after day. A great contributor to helping maintain a motivated team is _____, _____, _____ communication.

Retaining good employees has everything to do with the manager's ability to foster positive, meaningful communication. It is important to all of us to:

_____

_____

_____

_____

Besides providing information on what is expected, progress to goals, etc., communication also means _____ to our employees.

If you communicate with each member of your team in a similar fashion, you are practicing _____ _____.

One tool to help you save time and help everyone on your team improve current performance would be to prepare together a
P_____ I _____ A_____ P_____.

Meeting with employees to discuss performance can be done meaningfully in very little time. It is recommended **at least**:

Once a _____ for at and above-expectation performers

Once a _____ for below-expectation performers.

It is acceptable for people to be non-performers because you just do not have the time to meet with them all.   True or False: _____

Whose responsibility is it to measure and communicate? _____.

Check your answers on the next page.

What have you learned so far? (Answers)

Four ingredients of how to improve your team's performance:

a. Training

b. Coaching

c. Measuring

d. Communicating

What is the difference between measuring and communicating?

Measuring is <u>the objective tracking of progress toward an expected standard or outcome.</u>

Communicating is <u>the means of sharing information, expectations, status, and results.</u>

Most members of your team need your help to stay motivated day after day. A great contributor to helping maintain a motivated team is <u>frequent, consistent, meaningful</u> communication.

Retaining good employees has everything to do with the manager's ability to foster positive, meaningful communication. It is important to all of us to:

<u>Know what is expected.</u>

<u>Know how we are doing relative to those expectations.</u>

<u>Have a clear understanding of the importance of our role in helping the company meet or exceed the customer's expectations.</u>

Besides providing information on what is expected, progress to goals, etc., communication also means <u>listening</u> to our employees.

If you communicate with each member of your team in a similar fashion, you are practicing <u>communication consistency</u>.

One tool to help you save time and help everyone on your team improve current performance would be to prepare together a <u>*Performance Improvement Action Plan.*</u>

Meeting with employees to discuss performance can be done meaningfully in very little time. It is recommended <u>at least</u>:

Once a <u>quarter</u> for at and above-standard performers

Once a <u>week</u> for below-standard performers

It is acceptable for people to be non-performers because you just do not have the time to meet with them all. <u>False</u>

Whose responsibility is it to measure and communicate? <u>The manager.</u>

How Prepared Are You to Communicate?

On a scale of 1 to 10 (10 = highest) rate yourself on how well you do each of the following:

Rating

_____ I ensure my team knows the team goals and performance expectations.

_____ I give a positive greeting to everyone I come in contact with when I arrive at work in the morning.

_____ When any member of my team wants to talk with me, I make time to listen, even if means scheduling time to do it.

_____ When listening to an employee's needs or concerns, I listen intently and paraphrase back the points I heard to be sure I understood properly.

_____ I treat all employees consistently and do not play favorites, even though it is hard sometimes.

_____ I compliment a team member publicly when a task is done right.

_____ When I see an incorrect behavior, I take a team member aside and remind her/him of the correct behavior.

_____ Any time team interaction needs to be smoothed out, I meet with the team to discuss how more effective interaction can improve the team's ability to meet expectations and achieve goals.

_____ I make sure team members know I am there to listen if they need help.

_____ I ensure employees know how they are measured and report to them their status and progress toward reaching or exceeding expectations at least monthly.

_____ **TOTAL** ÷ 10 = _____.

Circle your score:

1--1.5--2--2.5--3--3.5--4--4.5--5--5.5--6--6.5--7--7.5--8--8.5--9--9.5--10

Not Prepared   Somewhat Prepared   Well Prepared

Success Factor 3:
Conduct Reviews Often, Fairly, Positively, and On Time

Managers should always be in the process of training and coaching their people, meeting frequently (daily, weekly, monthly or quarterly, depending upon need) to continuously develop their staff. Good coaching means the manager and individual regularly work together on specific action plans to improve performance in particular areas. Coaching provides the important opportunity to keep each team member aware of her/his performance and helps ensure expectations are being met on a continuing basis.

Effective managers do not wait for the formal review to sit down and talk candidly with an individual about her/his performance and write up action plans accordingly. They are doing this critical part of their job constantly as part of the coaching process and placing copies of the completed coaching action plans in each individual's personnel file for reference when the next formal review is due.

Good managers communicate their expectations and keep good records of how each employee is meeting, exceeding or falling below those expectations. These managers know how hard it is to accurately remember all the important information about each employee's performance, so they set aside a few minutes daily or weekly for new employees and monthly to quarterly for all others to reflect and document progress. These managers also know how valuable it is for employees to measure their own performance.

For managers who communicate with their team regularly about behavior, attitude and the quality and quantity of work to be done, performance reviews are "no surprise" and most often positive experiences.

A tool that helps many managers and their employees keep track of performance is the *Performance Improvement Action Plan*. Managers must strive to stay focused on behavior associated with meeting each standard of performance, while staying objective and consistent. These written plans help accomplish this.

Consistent use of *Performance Improvement Action Plans* to document performance and development sets the stage for the performance review and helps to eliminate unpleasant surprises.

Conducting the performance review plays an important role in the positive development of each employee. Sometimes managers mistakenly believe that the performance review is just another coaching session. It is critical to understand the difference before moving on.

Coaching is the **process** of guiding and developing an employee's performance to reach and exceed the expectations set for the job. The process includes:

- Ensuring proper training is provided to learn required skills.

- Continuously observing and measuring performance on the job.

- Working action plans with each employee focused on bringing performance to or above standard.

- Openly recognizing above-standard performance/behavior.

- Privately counseling below-standard performance/behavior.

- Privately disciplining improper performance/behavior.

Conducting a performance review is an **event.** It is a special time a manager sets aside with the employee to:

- Review overall performance to standard and results of *Performance Improvement Action Plans* since the last review.

- Discuss personal growth goals related to the job and the business.

- Possibly change earnings based upon performance.

There is a significant difference between coaching and conducting a performance review and yet they are both necessary components of good management. They work in harmony with each other. All of us have strengths and weaknesses. At any stage in an employee's lifecycle at work, coaching should be taking place to assist in improving weak areas and building upon strengths. It is coaching (planned, written, worked on, and measured) that provides the ingredients for a successful performance review.

The performance review is a special, timed event reserved for:

- Employees in training who are progressing toward meeting expectations

- Employees who are successfully working an action plan and are progressing to standard performance according to plan

- Employees who consistently have met or exceeded expectations since their last review

This is a *review* event **NOT** a *surprise* event. There should be no surprises.

When a position becomes available or needs to be created and an existing employee has the best qualifications and personality traits for the position, this may be the time for a promotion, **NOT** a performance review.

When an employee's performance is consistently below standard, and action plans clearly document limited or non-progress, this may be the time for termination **NOT** a performance review. When poor performers (consistent performance below standard) are allowed to remain as part of your team, you are not being fair to them, everyone else on your team, and most of all, yourself. Some of the most damaging outcomes of retaining a poor performer are:

- Your performance expectations are lowered.

- Your goal is placed in jeopardy.

- Good performers' morale suffers because they have to compensate for poor performers.

What have you learned so far?

What are the three management success factors?

_____

_____

_____

What are performance expectations? _____

List two of the most serious consequences of accepting consistent below-standard performance:

1. _____   2. _____

When bringing in new hires, it is very helpful to discuss with them three expectations-related issues:

_____

_____

_____

Expectations that are usually tied to some numeric result – like how much, how many, how often – are considered _____ expectations.

Expectations that relate to specific criteria or parameters – like how good, how efficient, how flexible – are considered _____ expectations.

Performance expectations must be:

a. Clear
b. Simple to communicate
c. Measurable
d. Lead to desired results
e. All of the above

Can you remember the three values associated with excellent attendance discussed in chapter 1?

1. _____

2. _____

3. _____

From chapter 1, what are three attitude performance expectations most successful work teams adhere to:

1. _____

2. _____

3. _____

What is the value of having performance expectations for attitude?_____

_____

Check your answers on the next page.

What have you learned so far? (Answers)

What are the three management success factors?

Recruit and hire the best people for the job.

Train and coach everyone to meet the performance expectations of the job, promoting consistently standard or above-standard performers and terminating consistently below-standard performers.

Conduct performance reviews fairly, positively and in a timely manner.

What are performance expectations? <u>State what is expected in a job and how it will be measured.</u>

List two of the most serious consequences of accepting consistent below-standard performance:

a. Not reach goal   b. Increase expenses

When bringing in new hires, it is very helpful to discuss with them three expectations-related issues:

<u>Expectations of the job and which ones apply immediately.</u>

<u>Which expectations have a learning period and what to expect during that period.</u>

<u>What training and assistance will be provided to ensure a new hire has the opportunity to reach standard in the normal time frame.</u>

Expectations that are usually tied to some numeric result like how much, how many, how often are considered <u>quantity</u> expectations.

Expectations that relate to specific criteria or parameters – like how good, how efficient, how flexible – are considered <u>quality</u> expectations.

Performance expectations must be: **e.** All of the above

Can you remember the three values associated with excellent attendance discussed in chapter 1?

1. Ensures each member of the team is pulling her/his weight

2. Shows respect for team

3. Shows respect and importance of one's own work

From chapter 1, what are three attitude performance expectations most successful work teams adhere to:

Right to be heard.

Right to be treated respectfully.

Right to express ideas.

What is the value of having performance expectations for attitude? Can help lead to appropriate team interaction and communication.

Determining Increase Awards

Increase amounts can easily be based upon expectations met or expectations exceeded. Percentages can be assigned to the expectations that, when totaled, yield the percentage increase for that employee.

An increase is a reward for past performance, not future expectations. The only exceptions to this might include an increase given for a promotion or a job that has changed to include more work and responsibility.

Most salespeople are paid commission and can dictate their own increases in earnings by increasing their sales revenue volume. For those in hourly or salaried positions, the annual performance review often carries expectations of an increase. If an increase is awarded, let the employee know during the review what the increase is and when she/he should expect to see the increase reflected in her/his paycheck. If the review is late for any reason and an increase has been warranted and approved, gain your manager's approval, and then let the employee know the increase will be retroactive "as of" the actual date the review should have been conducted.

It is best to contact your manager or the payroll department to confirm how and when increases will be effective and paid. Be sure to ask when all necessary review forms must be turned in to ensure the increase goes through as planned.

If a special increase arrangement was approved and the requirements of the arrangement were satisfied, the increase should be effective according to that arrangement. Hopefully, you will have documentation on file to support any special arrangement. It is very uncomfortable for a new manager to inherit a special arrangement that has no documentation to support it.

No or poor documentation is often a sign of an inexperienced, poorly trained and coached manager or one who does not take her/his people responsibilities seriously. Unfortunately, these are the same managers who tend to make the job more difficult than it needs to be for themselves, their team, and the company.

By simply adding two columns to the *Performance Expectation Sheet* we discussed in chapter 1, an increase table is created to record how increases are planned for and will be paid out. S and AS, respectively, stand for consistent standard (meets expectations) or above standard (exceeds expectations) performance since last review.

An example of an increase table appears on the next page. This is one method for ensuring pay increases can be fairly and consistently given. Higher percentages are placed where there is an opportunity to beat the standard, i.e., lower absenteeism, higher revenue. If increases are awarded to standard and above-standard performers only, with usually higher awards going to the above-standard performers, you have just eliminated a big problem a manager faces – justifying no or a low increase to an employee who is consistently performing below standard and who knows other below-standard performers got raises.

Be consistent in your reviews, as consistency is the key to good management.

Increase Table for Invoicing Clerk

Responsibilities

Performance Expectations
Quantity & Quality

Increase%
Standard | Above Standard

Responsibilities	Performance Expectations	Standard	Above Standard
Attendance	1. Less than 2 late arrivals, early leaves or absences per quarter or less than 5 total per year. Illness or absence requiring additional time should be discussed with your manager.	.5	1.0
Attitude	2. Uphold team members' rights to be: Heard Treated respectfully Given opportunities to express ideas	.5	.5
Meet Processing Goals (Exception: new hire will consistently meet standard within 10 working days.)	3. Average Invoice Processing Time Retail 20 per hr Wholesale 12 per hr Invoicing Reports 10 per hr	1.5	4.0
Accuracy	4. Error Rate < 1%	.5	.5
Measure & Communicate (Progress to goal, performance to expectations.)	5. Know your & the overall team goals and status 6. Know your Performance Expectations and status daily/weekly/monthly	.5 .5	.5 .5
	Maximum Base Increase Percentage Available	4%	7%

There is no reward for performance below expectation.
If rep meets expectations 1,4,5 and exceeds on 3 but is below standard on 2 & 6, what % would this rep's increase be? (Did you come up with 5.5?)

Preparing to Conduct the Performance Review

Your calendar is a great place to schedule when performance reviews are due for each employee. The first day a new employee attends work is a great day to mark your calendar for the first review due. On the day the first review is accomplished, automatically mark your calendar for the next review. This way you never forget.

There are five planning steps in preparing for the performance review.

1. See your Performance Review Checklist (next page) and plan what you want to accomplish.

2. Plan review meeting to occur on or no later than due date (check employee's schedule).

3. Plan time for both you and your employee to gather performance, progress, and future plan information before the review (gather all needed information).

4. Plan to conduct an on-time review (demonstrates courtesy and importance).

5. Plan to keep an open and honest dialogue (demonstrates leadership and management ability).

At least one week before review is due give your employee:

*   Confirmation of review meeting date/time/place (schedule conference room if needed).

*   Self-evaluation form to complete and return to you 2 days before the review.

*   A Titletown example self-evaluation form is provided after the checklist.

Performance Review Checklist

Did I set the stage?

_____ Ensured team member knew performance expectations.

_____Trained steps, tasks, and procedures required to meet or exceed standard.

_____Coached to perform each step, task, and procedure at or above standard.

_____Coached immediately to any change in expectations.

_____ Kept aware of her/his own performance to standard.

_____ Consistently, publicly recognized any above-standard performance and documented it.

_____ Consistently, privately counseled and disciplined any below-standard performance and documented it.

Am I prepared for the review?

_____ Planned what the review must accomplish.

_____ Scheduled thirty to sixty minutes for review on or near actual due date.

_____ Scheduled prep time at least three business days prior to review.

_____ Notified employee of review date; gave employee self-evaluation form.

_____ Kept my assigned preparation date and completed all associated tasks.

_____ Considerately set quiet, private, comfortable place; will arrive a little ahead and be ready to greet. (Avoid conducting a performance review while sitting behind your desk. A conference room can be a great alternative.)

Did I complete the review process?

_____ Welcomed employee to the event.

_____ Maintained a positive and professional manner.

_____Stayed on track and completed review.

_____ Completed all information required on the review form.

_____ Signed the review as did the employee.

_____Placed completed and signed review form and all supporting documentation in employee's personnel file.

Am I following up?

Example Self-Evaluation Form

Name: _____   Position: _____   Date: _____

Please rate yourself to the expected expectations.

Responsibilities	Quantity & Quality Performance Expectations (measurable)	Avg Status Below Meet Above	Change in performance and/or responsibilities since last review.
Attendance	Less than 1 late arrival, early leave or absence per quarter or less than 4 total per year. Illness or absence requiring additional time should be discussed with your manager.		
Attitude	Uphold team members' rights to be: Heard, Treated respectfully, Given opportunities to express ideas.		
Meet revenue Expectations	$5,000 wk Avg. sale $650 (Min. 8 avg. or above avg. sales per wk) Less than 5% total receivables over 60 days Maintain 8+ customer satisfaction rating.		
Submit sales reports to manager	On time and 100% accuracy Weekly Sales to Plan Report due Mon. 10am. Monthly sales by industry/product due 2 business days after mo. end.		
Measure & communicate progress to goal, performance to Expectations	Know your & the overall team goals and status. Know your Performance Expectations and status daily/weekly/monthly) Can define how you are measured Can tie your compensation to performance expectations.		

Action Plan in progress: Y ___ N ___. (Please attach copies of all action plans completed or in process since last review date.)

Additional review forms or back-up information: (Please staple to back of this form as needed.) Additional attached Y/ N ___ .

Additional Comments: _____

Keep your preparation date.

- Review all notes since last review in employee's personnel file.

- Action plans should be in file along with dated performance/coaching notes.

- Complete *Performance Review Form* and compare your responses to employee's self-evaluation.

- Determine where you rated employee higher (good news, move on).

- Determine where you rated employee same (good news, move on).

- Determine where you rated employee lower than her/his rating (employee needs your help, spend time here).

Clear, shared performance expectations help avoid troublesome inconsistencies.

- Check to see that your ratings reflect average performance over entire time period, not just yesterday's good or bad behavior.

- Obtain any needed approval and effective dates for any compensation change.

- The day before the review, call to remind employee of place and time.

- Ask employee to come prepared with her/his performance averages for each standard since last review.

- Tell employee you are looking forward to this time together.

Conduct the review as planned and file all paperwork promptly. The *Performance Review Form* is provided in the forms section in the back of the book.

Special Thoughts for the First Review

During an employee's first forty-five days to six months on the job, depending upon the job complexity, training and coaching should be occurring at least weekly and in many cases daily. If an employee is on target, consistently meeting expectations, the first three- or six-month performance review should be a simple and positive event. If the employee has not met standard within the average and possibly additional time allotted, given training and coaching, termination may be considered rather than a review.

What if the employee is steadily progressing, but is still performing below average and there are concerns? Discussions and documented development plans along the way help to prevent surprises. A well-prepared manager can conduct a caring, professional, open, and honest discussion of what is expected, by when, and the results of meeting and maintaining the expectations or not meeting them. This exchange can help the employee clarify her/his own goals to ensure they match the needs of the position. Remember, expectations are there to help your team succeed. Everyone's ability to perform at standard is the minimum expectation all of you should have. Everyone just may not get there at exactly the same time.

Be sure to follow the five planning steps discussed in the section titled **Preparing to Conduct the Performance Review** and add these few ingredients to assist in this special first review:

- Ensure the employee understands the performance expectations and the review process.

- Using the pre-prepared self-evaluation and your own completed evaluation form, discuss and come to agreement on where performance is to standard.

- If below standard and still in the normal training period:

  - Provide needed training and together write up an action plan to help reach standard in the time expected. (You are willing to help.)

  - Set dates and times to train and coach. (You do help.)

- Be clear when each expectation is to be reached. (The employee has to make it happen.)

• If at or above standard, and any wage increase was promised contingent upon this, confirm the employee has earned the increase and let her/him know when it will become effective.

How Prepared Are You to
Conduct a Performance Review?

On a scale of 1 to 10 (10 = highest) rate yourself on how well you do each of the following:

Rating

_____ I ensure my team knows the performance expectations.

_____ I learn from my direct reports, at least weekly, where we are in relation to expectations, why and what actions are being taken to ensure expectations will continue to be met or exceeded.

_____ Any time an individual's attitude, attendance or work performance is above standard, I praise them and when below standard, I counsel them.

_____ I jot down a note or document on a current action plan, when I see behavior consistently above standard and keep it on file so I won't forget.

_____ When any individual's performance is below standard, I determine if training, coaching or counseling may be needed and act on it.

_____ I jot down a note or document on a current action plan any individual's consistently below-standard behavior and keep it on file so I won't forget.

_____ I let the new hires know what is expected of them by when, and work closely with them to train, coach, and monitor progress in that time frame.

_____ Any time an individual's performance falls below standard I discuss with the person what she/he is doing or needs to do to get back on track.

_____ When an individual is performing consistently above standard, I work with this person to creatively keep her/him feeling challenged.

_____ My employee turnover rate is below company average.

_____ TOTAL ÷ 10 = _____.   Circle your score:

1--1.5--2--2.5--3--3.5--4--4.5--5--5.5--6--6.5--7--7.5--8--8.5--9--9.5--10

Not Prepared   Somewhat Prepared   Well Prepared

Consideration starts first with the manager believing in and consistently practicing the three success factors. Believe it or not, reviews are often a tense time for many employees. This is mainly because not all managers adhere to some of the fundamental practices described in this coaching guide and the employee is left anxious and unprepared. Just think what it would be like to work for a few months and not know if you are doing a good job. You are told you are doing fine but you are just not sure. This often happens when you do not know what the expectations are or the manager communicates them but seems to interpret them differently for each member of the team. For instance, you know there are team members who perform consistently below standard because you often have to do more work to make up for them. Yet one of them had a review last month and got a nice raise. Another, who is a good friend and lunch buddy of the manager, was just promoted.

The second major point of consideration comes when our review date is approaching. Most of us know when our review is due. It is an important date to most of us. If it is an annual review, and you are not in sales, where you often control your own pay increases by selling more and earning more commission, this is usually the time you expect to receive a pay increase. Well, the due date comes and goes and your manager doesn't say a word. If this has ever happened to you, you understand the feeling. It is a wise habit to keep review due dates on your calendar and adhere to them.

A third way to show consideration is by conducting the review in a quiet, private place where you both can sit comfortably. Public places like restaurants are not ideal to conduct a review. A quiet conference room or your office, if you have a worktable with two chairs, can be an ideal setting. Conducting a review in a place where others can hear and be heard, or phone calls constantly interrupt the manager, sends the wrong message to the employee and diminishes the importance of this special event. Think of yourself in your own review and your manager is sitting behind her/his desk. How do you feel? Often people say they feel intimidated or set apart when seated face to face with the desk between them. Even if the manager doesn't mean for it to be intimidating, perception is reality, and most people feel uncomfortable.

The fourth way to show consideration is to have with you the employee's completed self-evaluation, your completed review form, and all action plans completed during the review time period and in progress currently. Both you and the employee should know her/his average performance to standard since the last review.

Lastly, the fifth consideration means arriving a little ahead of time to be ready to greet your employee and help get the review off to a good start. Help the employee get comfortable.

5 key considerations were discussed on the last page that mean a lot when conducting a performance review. Can you remember what they are (try not to look back)?

1. _____

2. _____

3. _____

4. _____

5. _____

If expectations are simple, measurable, and have been openly communicated, you have eliminated one of the biggest problems a manager faces – reviewing an employee who believes her/his performance is better than you believe it is.

By consistently using *Performance Improvement Action Plans* to document performance and development, especially when performance is below standard, you eliminate the problem of trying to gain agreement on poor performance and attempting to correct it during the performance review rather than when the poor performance actually occurs.

If increases are awarded to standard and above-standard performers only, with higher awards going to above-standard performers, you do not have to concern yourself with justifying no increase to an employee who is consistently performing below standard and yet knows other below-standard employees got raises.

Walking Through a Review

Here is an example of how a manager, using the principles taught in this coaching guide, might progress through a typical review. Remember, this manager would not wait for the review date to promote someone who qualifies for a desired position or wait for or use the performance review to terminate a consistently below-standard performer.

START WITH A POSITIVE CLARIFYING STATEMENT

"Thank you, *Mary*, for joining me to review your performance since your last review and to discuss goals and plans for the future. I've been looking forward to this important time together."

ALWAYS DISCUSS AT- OR ABOVE-STANDARD RATINGS FIRST

"Let's start by focusing on where you rated yourself on your self-evaluation form at or above standard. We'll start with the first one. Tell me what you believe have been your most positive experiences and improvements in this particular area.

Remain quiet and listen. When given a one-line or incomplete response, say, "Tell me more."

After obtaining the employee's response on that responsibility, share your positive rating and why you rated her/him that way. Be honest and considerate at all times.

Repeat the sequence for each, until all of the responsibilities in this standard/ above-standard category are addressed.

DISUCSS BELOW-STANDARD RATINGS NEXT:

"We all have strengths and we all have needs areas where we can improve. That is why we use action plans. Let's review your current *Performance Improvement Action Plan* and make sure it covers any below-standard areas we want to focus on improving."

REVIEW PLAN IN PROGRESS TOGETHER:

Ensure any areas below standard are listed on the plan and add what is not.

Determine understanding and commitment by asking:

"Why do you believe it is important these expectations exist and are maintained?"

Remain quiet and listen. When given a one-line or incomplete response, say, "Tell me more."

Discuss any barrier that the employee believes is standing in the way of consistently being able to perform at standard.

Work on solutions to these barriers together and update the plan as needed.

Be honest and considerate at all times.

DISUCSS ANY INCREASE NEXT

"Mary, let's take a look at your average performance against each standard since your last review. On the review form are those familiar performance expectations to be met or exceeded. Let's compare your overall performance to those expectations. How did you do in each area of responsibility?"

You requested in your reminder call yesterday for Mary to have this ready, and you have it as well.

Let the employee report her/his findings. Confirm or correct these findings as you go to ensure accuracy (use reports). If the expectations changed, reports should have changed simultaneously to reflect the new expectations so no confusion exists. You are ready to proceed.

"Overall your average performance numbers since your last review show that you have consistently exceeded standard in these two areas, met five of these expectations, and performed below standard in only one area.

If you use the increase table, show it to the employee. She/he should be familiar with it.

"This is wonderful because it means you earned an increase for your good work. What does your increase % come out to be? (Work with the employee to come to the correct %.)

"That % translates to $_____ more per pay period. The effective date is your review due date, which happens to be today. You will see the increase in your next check. Any questions or concerns before we move on?" Address any questions/concerns completely before moving on if appropriate at this time. Be honest and considerate at all times.

NOW COMES THE TIME TO DISCUSS FUTURE GOALS AND PLANS

"Well, Mary, I'd now like to turn our attention to the future. You are a valued member of this team and this company so I am very interested in your goals and plans for this next year. Are you comfortable discussing this topic with me today?

If the response is no, do not press. "Please let me know when you are ready. I am very interested in where you see yourself in your career." If the response is yes, remain quiet and listen.

Make notes of the goals and plans discussed on the review form. Share any requirements you are aware of associated with reaching the goals and plans. If a goal is to move into another area in the company, ask the employee if she/he has talked to the head of that department to learn what the hiring criteria are. If not, encourage them to do so. Assure employee of your support on moving to another area as long as performance averages standard or above. Be honest and considerate at all times.

CONCLUDING THE REVIEW

"We have reviewed your performance since your last review, *your increase*, and your goals and plans for the future. Is there anything else you wish to discuss before we close this review?"

Address any issues before moving on if appropriate at this time. Be honest and considerate at all times. Go over the completed review form with the employee and both of you sign it. Stand up, shake your employee's hand and say thank you for preparing and participating in this important event.

Your Thoughts on This Review Example

How do you feel about this review?

_____

_____

What occurred that is the same or similar to reviews you conduct?

_____

_____

What occurred that is different from reviews you conduct?

_____

_____

From now on what might you do differently and why?

_____

_____

Jones and Jones Case:

The Jones and Jones inside sales department's manager, John prides himself on making all his new employees attend orientation the first day of work.

He trains everyone on the use of the computer and the phone system. Occasionally he even coaches some of the poor performers in how to handle calls more effectively. At least once a month, John tells the three top performers they are being counted on to exceed the 20% up-sell standard to ensure the team meets monthly revenue goals.

Julie, one of the sales reps, has been with the company for two years and in the last six months has been consistently tardy or absent. In the last two months, she has been absent three Fridays and late two Mondays. On only one occasion was the reason illness. When she is at work all five days, she often exceeds the 20% up-sell standard by 5% or more.

Last week John gave Julie her annual performance review. He told her how pleased he was with her up-sell ability. He even asked her if she was interested in possibly becoming a group leader to help the below-standard performers. He never mentioned the absenteeism performance expectation but suggested she do something about her lateness and absenteeism, as the other reps were complaining. All Julie's reviews cite her as a good performer. Last week's review was the first time anything was said about absences but nothing was noted on the review form. John gave Julie a raise.

Julie feels good about her review and even believes a promotion is coming soon. John, relieved the review is over, got angry when Julie came in late the Monday following the review because her alarm didn't go off. He thought, "I've heard that one before. I better write this down." He was so busy he forgot.

NOTE: Immediately after the review, John was called back to putting out fires, so he put Julie's review forms in his bottom drawer until he could get back to his desk. Julie's review forms were forgotten about. A week later when she saw no raise in her paycheck, Julie went screaming to John's manager, saying John should be fired for promising a raise and not giving it.

What does John do right and/or wrong?

_____

What concerns might you have about Julie?

_____

What concerns might you have for the team?

_____

If you were John's manager, what would you do to help John? _____

_____

Coaching Your Way to Success

Success for an aggressive, growth-oriented business requires a management process that stimulates productivity and flexibility. It is all about how good we are at bringing others forward to meet the demands of innovation and changing expectations. The coaching method described in this book focuses on three management success factors that make that happen:

1. Recruiting and hiring the best people for the job.

2. Training and coaching all to meet the performance expectations of the job.

3. Conducting performance reviews often, fairly, positively, and on time.

In the finely woven fabric of management, coaching is the most significant thread. With the aid of this coaching guide, the four forms, and your clearly communicated expectations, you can be off and running. Expect positive and significant results. When the process is fully implemented, results are normally evident within ninety days and continue as long as the process is in use.

The simple management principles and methods discussed in this book can be trained to and implemented quickly. Just refer to the book as often as you need to. Your HR executive can determine the best way to incorporate the principles and forms into employee relations, training, and HR systems.

Although there are many sample tools provided that you are welcome to use, there are only four critical forms that are required to make it work.

-   **Performance Expectations Sheet**

-   **Recruiting & Hiring Worksheet**

-   **Performance Review Form**

-   **Performance Improvement Action Plan**

The forms must be used completely and consistently. Whenever possible, program them into your HR system for easy entry, collection, and storage of information. Establish access codes as needed. Unless there is a very good reason to add more, do your best to limit completed forms required in a personnel file to these four only.

If you think this all sounds too simple, it is and it isn't. The process is simple. Making it happen depends on top-down desire and commitment. If you are limited financially, just ask all managers to read and follow the book using the four critical forms provided. Then spend everything else you have on teaching your senior executives how to coach and expect them to teach and coach all managers they support. Utilize the best coaching professionals, whether they are HR professionals well trained in the coaching process, or a third-party professional executive coach.

Creating a coaching culture can take less time than you think. Results are predicated on top-down buy-in, full process implementation and getting and giving as much coaching assistance as possible to all executives and managers in the organization. There is a direct correlation between quantity and quality of coaching and the results you achieve.

The straightforward, plain talk, "how to" instructions are for all to practice and refer to as often as needed. Just before you begin to recruit or coach or train or conduct a performance review, read the relevant chapter. As improvement occurs, continue to refer to the book as a reminder of what is important.

When all is said and done, what you have read and hopefully will implement, translates into a very simple concept.

Management's job is to set reasonable expectations, train and coach to those expectations, and measure and communicate along the way to reaching them.

We succeed if our people succeed.

Required Forms

1. Performance Expectation Sheet

2. Recruiting & Hiring Worksheet

3. Performance Review Form

4. Performance Improvement Action Plan

Forms used in this book may be copied or recreated and tailored to your company's needs.

Performance Expectations Sheet

Position Title:_____

Date:_____

Responsibilities	Quantity & Quality Performance Expectations

*Forms used in this book may be copied or recreated and
tailored to your company's needs.*

Recruiting & Hiring Worksheet

Position: _____ Applicant Name: _____

Interviewer: _____ Date: _____

	Phone Screen 1= exceeds 2= meets 3= below	1st Interview 1= exceeds 2= meets 3= below	2nd Interview 1= exceeds 2= meets 3= below
"MUST HAVE" Needs Assessment			
Qualifications (job description and your preferences):			
Personality Traits (characteristics of those successful in position):			

Forms may be copied or recreated and tailored to your company's needs.

Performance Review Form

Name: _____   Position: _____

Responsibilities	Quantity & Quality Performance Expectations (measurable)	Avg Status Below Meets Above	Change in performance & responsibilities since last review.

Action Plan in progress: Y ___ N____ (Please attach copies of all action plans completed or in process since last review.)

Please attach any **additional information or back-up information:**
Additional attached Y___ N___

Additional Comments:
_____
_____
_____

An increase has been approved Yes ___ No _____ If yes, amount of increase:_____

Employee's Signature _____ Date _____
Manager's Signature:_____ Date_____

Forms may be copied or recreated and tailored to your company's needs.

Performance Improvement Action Plan

Participant Name/Title _____ / _____

Manager Name _____

Plan Initiation Date ___/___/___ (Recommend no more than 3 goals at a time.)

Goals (1 goal per box)	Current Performance To Standard (Below, Meets, Above)	Specific Target Performance Desired.	Action Steps to Take to Reach Goal	Help I Need & From Whom	Date to Goal	Follow-up session Date / Results
						Date: Results:
						Date: Results:
						Date: Results:

Forms used in this book may be copied or recreated and tailored to your company's needs.

About the Author

A pioneer in the field of executive coaching, Dr. Capobianco has guided organizations through major business and cultural transformations. Utilizing a self-developed coaching-based method, she has led several start-ups and reorganizations, turning these entities into high performance, profitable, sustaining businesses. Her success was repeated over many years in various industries, including financial services, manufacturing, retail, publishing and communications.

Ms. Capobianco holds a Ph. D. in Organizational Development & Training and served as adjunct professor with Old Dominion University's Center for Global Business and Executive Education. She currently offers practical and effective management development workshops, one-on-one executive coaching and is a highly applauded motivational speaker on subjects of leadership, coaching and getting through change quickly and successfully.